Praise for Michael Eric Dyson

"Michael Eric Dyson . . . is a world-class scholar and the most brilliant interpreter of hip hop culture we have."
   Jay Z

"If any one person is continuing W. E. B. Du Bois's idea of the engaged public intellectual on African-American issues, it's Michael Eric Dyson."
   Steven Nadler, *Professor of Philosophy,*
   University of Wisconsin

"The preeminent black intellectual."
   The Boston Phoenix

"Few have carried on the legacy of Du Bois's public intellectualism as well, or with as much verve . . . as Professor Michael Eric Dyson."
   Lawrence Bobo, *the W. E. B. Du Bois Professor*
   of the Social Sciences at Harvard University

"The ideal public intellectual for our time: translator, boundary-breaker, and healer of a war torn culture."
   Naomi Wolff

"Michael Eric Dyson is reshaping what it means to be a public intellectual by becoming the most visible black academic of his time."
   The Philadelphia Weekly

"Such is the genius of Dyson. He flows freely from the profound to the profane, from popular culture to classical literature."
   Washington Post

To

Ingrid Saunders Jones
Richard Plepler
Johnny Furr
Mike Bantom
Kenneth Chenault
and
Marva Smalls

Gifted Executives,
Good Friends
and Great Americans

Contents

Telling the Truth Gently

Dave Eggers

"Tell the truth gently." This maxim ends this book, but I'm making sure it opens it too. It characterizes, though doesn't summarize, Michael Eric Dyson's work and the wall-to-wall aphoristic wisdom this book collects. It's very hard to both tell the truth and do it with care, but Dyson has proved himself master of this high-wire act. He's an electrifying man of words — this is clear to anyone who has read him or heard him or seen him speak. Although he is entirely unafraid to walk into a rhetorical firefight, he is careful, he is considered, and he always seeks peaceful resolution to any debate, no matter how fraught. His ability to clarify complex and painful issues with lyrical prose, all the while avoiding cheap shots or opening new wounds, is remarkable. While Dyson makes it look easy, it's exceedingly difficult. It's very hard to both tell the truth and do it with care. As he puts it himself: "Paying attention to how you say what you say doesn't mean you have nothing to say."

Can You Hear Me Now? is being published at the beginning of what many of us hope is a new era of magnanimity. President Obama has stunned and energized a conflict-weary nation with his willingness to embrace his erstwhile opponents, and the ever-widening embrace he models for us has allowed millions to reconsider the divisions in our own lives — in our communities, at our jobs, among family members. There exists the hope that through his example of generosity, notably married with intellectual curiosity, we will usher in a new period of honest and respectful dialogue, of candor, of listening with humility, an era where debate is conducted with vigor, honesty, and civility.

Michael Eric Dyson has been doing this for years. With his incredibly prolific pen, he's been speaking for the voiceless, explaining the inexplicable, putting to rest tired lies and unearthing new truths. No one has explained hip hop better. His examination of Colin Powell's life and what it signifies is pretty much definitive. His writing about the oratory of Martin Luther King, Jr., is unparalled. And in the aftermath of Hurricane Katrina, it was Dyson, perhaps more than anyone else, who put the government's criminal neglect into historical context, channeled our collective rage, and cleared a path forward.

I had the pleasure of publishing some of Dyson's early work at *Might*, a small magazine I started with some friends just after college. One day in the early '90s, one of our editors, Paul Tullis, was at a hip hop symposium in New York. He caught Dr. Dyson speaking on a panel, and he was astounded. As he does on most panels, Dyson blew everyone out of the room. Here was a professor of religion who was no stuffed shirt — he could quote Chuck D and the Wu Tang Clan one minute, Nietzsche and Hegel the next, the words of scripture and Milton and MLK mixed in for good measure. And he could do it all with great flow, disarming humor, and insanely quick wit. Nothing could sound more leaden than a panel discussion on hip hop, but Dyson, through sheer force of will and facility with words, was able to bring it to life. This is the mark of a born writer.

Tullis approached him after the panel, asking him if he wanted to write a column for our little magazine. Dyson already had a national reputation, but he was young enough that Tullis felt it was at least worth a shot. We could pay very little, Tullis said, but maybe Dyson wanted to reach the kind of people who were reading our magazine — that is, young idealists with a sense of humor? When Dyson said yes, we were thrilled, but we also had that moment of confused insecurity that inspired Groucho Marx's quote: "I wouldn't want to belong to a club that would have me." Why would Michael Eric Dyson agree to appear in our two-bit magazine?

Watching his career since, the answer is clear. Dyson wants to talk to those who want to listen. In the interest of bringing light into the many dark corners of ignorance, he's faced the blowhard wrath of Bill O'Reilly and the grandfatherly chiding of Bill Cosby. And though Dyson's profile and reputation have grown every year, he's still the kind of guy who will take the time to talk to a young person looking to him for clarity and guidance. Type Dyson's name into YouTube and you'll find the professor, wearing a Yankees cap, being interviewed outside a Nas concert. It's obvious the young journalist who waylaid him is stunned that Dyson has stopped to talk to him, and in response to the interviewer's question — "Why are you seeing Nas tonight?" — Dyson lays down, off the top of his head, a wide-ranging and prose-perfect dissertation on the power and significance of Nas's music. The fact that Dyson would take the time to think about the interviewer's questions, and would get excited about talking about the answers, shows that he's a guy who wakes up in the morning wanting to challenge and be challenged.

If you're equally willing to be challenged and enlightened, you're holding a precious volume. For the newcomer to

Dyson's work, it's a great primer, grabbing some of the best passages from his essays and books over the last eighteen years or so. For the longtime reader, it's a one-volume greatest hits package. Dyson's always been the kind of writer you read with highlighter in hand, ready to illuminate some sentence you could have sworn was written by Cicero or Douglass or Lincoln or King. So this book does the work for you. Try this one: "Justice is what love sounds like when it speaks in public." Or this: "Spirituality makes religion behave." That's Dyson at his most concise and aphoristic, but there are also the passages that give you new lenses through which to see an issue. Here's one of the best: "This is a painful paradox of race: that blacks must often be *rejected into* the American creed, that they are often included only after their alienation from America reveals America's alienation from its social ideals." It was Dyson who called Obama "a re-founding father," who called the O. J. Simpson trial a "racequake." It was Dyson who said, "Like a poisonous mushroom, the tangled assumptions of race grow best in darkness." And this: "One of the problems with neoliberalism is that it writes the check of its loyalty to the black and Latino poor against the funds of conservative rhetoric and social policy." I could go on quoting the man, but that's the point and task of the pages that follow.

The last point I'll make is that Dr. Dyson has a way of exploring complex issues full of contradiction and finding a way to leave the reader with a sense of clarity of vision — and even urgency of purpose. And the same could be said of the man. Michael Eric Dyson is alive to the fierce urgency of now and yet he's full of felicitous contradictions: an intellectual who won't talk down to anyone; a man of God who eschews piousness; a truth-teller who is not afraid of doubt or nuance; a fighter whose arguments, though always to the point, are never ad hominem. We can and should be thankful we have a writer like Michael Eric Dyson in our midst. And to have him at a time like this? Very interesting. In 1996 he wrote, "We can strive for a society where each receives his or her just due, where the past in all its glory and grief is part of the equation of racial justice and social equality. Then we won't need to be blind to color, which in any case is a most morbid state of existence. Then we can embrace our history and ideals with the sort of humane balance that makes democracy more than a distant dream." Is this that time? With Dyson's help, we shall see.

Can You Hear Me Now?

chapter 1

Obama

The distance from Martin Luther King's assassination to Barack Obama's inauguration is a quantum leap of racial progress whose timeline neither cynics nor boosters could predict.

Can You Hear Me Now?

Also by Michael Eric Dyson

April 4, 1968: Martin Luther King, Jr.'s Death and
How It Changed America (2008)

Know What I Mean? Reflections on Hip Hop (2007)

Debating Race with Michael Eric Dyson (2007)

Pride: The Seven Deadly Sins (2006)

Come Hell or High Water: Hurricane Katrina and
the Color of Disaster (2005)

Is Bill Cosby Right? Or Has the Black Middle Class
Lost Its Mind? (2005)

Mercy, Mercy Me: The Art, Loves, and Demons of Marvin Gaye (2004)

The Michael Eric Dyson Reader (2004)

Open Mike: Reflections on Philosophy, Race, Sex,
Culture, and Religion (2003)

Why I Love Black Women (2003)

Holler If You Hear Me: Searching for Tupac Shakur (2001)

I May Not Get There with You: The True Martin Luther King, Jr. (2000)

Race Rules: Navigating the Color Line (1997)

Between God and Gangsta Rap: Bearing Witness to
Black Culture (1996)

Making Malcolm: The Myth and Meaning of Malcolm X (1995)

Reflecting Black: African-American Cultural Criticism (1993)

Can You Hear Me Now?

The Inspiration,
Wisdom, and
Insight of

Michael Eric Dyson

BASIC
CIVITAS
BOOKS

A Member of the Perseus Books Group
New York

Published by Basic Civitas Books
A Member of the Perseus Books Group

Books published by Basic Civitas Books are available at special discounts for
bulk purchases in the United States by corporations, institutions, and other organizations. For more information, please contact the Special Markets Department at the Perseus Books Group, 2300 Chestnut Street, Suite 200, Philadelphia,
PA 19103, or call (800) 255-1514, or e-mail special.markets@perseusbooks.com.

Design by Jane Raese
Set in 10.5-point New Aster

Library of Congress Cataloging-in-Publication Data is available for this book.
ISBN 978-0-465-01883-3

10 9 8 7 6 5 4 3 2 1

If Barack Obama's emergence as the most powerful man in the world has not relieved the pull between color and country, it has proved that the black story is an American story.

Barack Obama is an *American* man; his triumph is an *American* moment.

In the adjectival way we measure racial progress, Obama is not a *black* president, but a black *president.*

Obama links his life to Abraham Lincoln's. He sees in the man he considers our greatest president the will to remake himself, and his surroundings, through imagination and hard work. You don't have to be what you used to be. You don't have to be trapped by a past that could simply be reshaped in the mirror of pitiless self-reflection. Such brilliant enthusiasm made fate a four-letter word. Just take destiny into your own hands — for Lincoln, by splitting rails, and for Obama, by toiling in communities — and then transform your labor into helpful policies through the law and politics.

Obama is the beneficiary of Frederick Douglass's eloquence and sense of struggle, Booker T. Washington's self-reliant uplift, W. E. B. Du Bois's brilliant unmasking of racial hierarchy, Mary McLeod Bethune's imperishable desire for education, Ella Baker's tactical and strategic energy, Malcolm X's will to literary reinvention, and Martin Luther King, Jr.'s soaring oratory and ultimate sacrifice. Obama is the latest link in the chain of progress they all forged in the struggle to improve the U.S. by improving the condition of black folk. Obama will move in exactly the opposite direction: As president, he will improve the condition of black folk because he improves the nation. That is a sign of his calling as a national leader, not a black leader.

If Obama had been successfully painted into a racial corner as "the black candidate," he would not only have lost his effectiveness as a viable contender in the mainstream, but he would have compromised the ability to uplift black constituents. If Obama couldn't get elected to help *all* Americans — and while black Americans were key to his election, blacks alone couldn't elect him — he couldn't get elected to help *any* Americans, including black Americans.

In 1968, the Rev. Martin Luther King, Jr., met a bullet in resistance to his dream of equality; forty years later, Americans cast their ballots to make Obama president. The distance from King's assassination to Obama's inauguration is a quantum leap of racial progress whose timeline neither cynics nor boosters could predict.

Contrary to many critics, his election does not, nor should it, herald a postracial future. But it may help usher in a *postracist* future. A postracial outlook seeks to delete crucial strands of our identity; a postracist outlook seeks to delete oppression that rests on hate and fear, and that exploits cultural and political vulnerability. Obama need not cease being a black man to effectively govern, but America must overcome its brutal racist past to permit his gifts, and those of other blacks, to shine.

It was awfully futile to string Obama up on a genetic tree and hang him for not being black enough, because, in the mother of all ironies, his mother is white and his father is African. The black folk claiming that he was not black the way they want him to be black — that he wasn't born of an American black father and mother — were pretty humorless and missed the irony of claiming that a black man born of immediate African ancestry didn't measure up to their test of blackness.

———

Our belief in Obama must become contagious; it must spread and become a belief in other blacks who have been quarantined in racial stereotype. Regarding Obama as an exceptional black man — when he is in fact an exceptional *American* — hampers our whole nation's desire to clear the path to success for more like him. Obama is not the first black American capable of being president; he's the first black American who got the chance to prove it.

———

Ever since he roared into our ears in eloquent cadence at the podium of the 2004 Democratic National Convention, Barack Obama has struck new chords in American politics. He has made millions believe that their elected leaders might dare to dream out loud and not mind saying so. He makes one feel that he can cast aside rigid categories and rise above the plodding aspirations that weigh down too many politicians. His written word sings; his spoken word soars on the wings of renewed faith in the democratic process, and how we need such renewal in an ugly age of despotic indifference to the freedom to think creatively. Obama's eyes are fixed on what we can make together of our national future.

One of the greatest effects of Obama's becoming the most powerful man in the world is the incalculable psychic boost it gives young black egos that take shape in the glare of TV screens that project his face and words around the globe. But the real miracle may be that Obama's presidency persuades Americans to take for granted that a talented black person, if trusted, can do a great deal of good for the country. Even before he swore his oath of office, Obama served the nation in heroic fashion.

Before he rose to fame, there was little doubt that Obama was black. He moved to the South Side of Chicago, home to black communities that have spawned sociological classics by Horace Cayton and St. Clair Drake, and William Julius Wilson. He took a low-paying job to work largely among the black poor. He joined the blackest church in town, for which he's taken considerable heat. He ran and lost a bid for Congress against an icon of sixties black struggle. He married a brilliant and beautiful and unmistakably black woman — for all, and for what, that's worth — with whom he is rearing two bright and lovely black daughters.

We should not be seduced by the notion that Obama's presidency signals the end of racism, the civil rights movement, the struggle for black equality or the careers of Jesse Jackson and Al Sharpton. A President Obama would not have come to be without the groundbreaking efforts of Shirley Chisholm, and especially Jackson. Obama is able to be cool and calm because leaders like Sharpton, at least in the past, got angry.

Obama taught the nation how being black is not a distortion of American ideals but rather a celebration of them. Still, Obama's foes tried to kick him to the curb of political life by demonizing him as a threat to the American way of life. He was bitterly denounced as a communist, socialist, Marxist, terrorist, traitor, and an un-American subversive. So Obama annoyed his critics by becoming even more American. He spoke of hope; he chastised bitter partisanship; he said his biracial roots gave him an understanding of all races; and he claimed his meteoric rise was possible only in America. Even as reports of foiled assassination plots surfaced, he continued to walk steadily toward the Oval Office with a steely resolve. In those moments, he owed as much to John Wayne as to Martin Luther King.

Obama's promise as a black man who bears none of the scorn or rancor of his civil rights predecessors is a double-edged razor: one of the reasons he's able to be the man he is — to have the noble bearing of a statesman who wants to get past the arguments of the past — is because those arguments were made, and bitter battles were fought, and in some cases, are still being fought.

Obama's belief in the American people is a reflection, in part, of the profound belief they have invested in him. His belief also greatly borrows from his trafficking in the cross-sections of various cultures, colors, and communities. Obama's roots in more than one race, and his experiences in many cultures, are not, as falsely advertised, a liability. But there has been a great deal of Obamanxiety; in fact, there's been a war in Barack, that is, in his metaphoric body, which captures the insular and insidious nature of so much talk about blackness and race.

Obama has the urgent sense of destiny that only a few politicians have ever truly possessed in American life. This is not to be confused with the gutless swagger of George W. Bush's revamped Manifest Destiny, or the perilous and bloated delusions of Richard Nixon.

Obama's restless self-reinventions — from organizer to state senator, from law professor to president of the United States — make him the very language of American social possibility. Obama the iconic figure has quickly come to express the idea that America could produce a man like him to lead the country forward in a time of nation-defining crisis. At first blush, all that Obama is *not* — a rich white man; the son of social royalty; a well-established Washington insider — makes him a counterintuitive choice to take the helm of a political vessel that threatens to capsize. Yet on closer inspection, it is precisely his mix of gifts that makes him the kind of man who can right the ship of American political destiny — a remarkably sober and cool demeanor, a keen intelligence and a political maturity far beyond his years, an eloquence drawn from fighting injustice, and a sensitivity to all sides of a debate born of his biracial heritage.

Obama is, no doubt, the product of a paradox: he rests atop an inverted racial pyramid that he has been credited with overturning, and yet without the fierce rumblings of race that his ascent seems to overcome, his career, and now his presidency, wouldn't necessarily be seen as the miracle of transcendence for which they've been touted.

The debate about whether or not Obama is black enough rested on a bad misreading of the politics of race in black America. That debate jumped off more in media than in the mouths of everyday black folk who longed to know more about Obama's politics, not his pigment.

The Oval Office is the ultimate symbol of national access to power. If the levers of influence are weighted with bias or unjust privilege, they swing away from the promise of democracy, which is America's greatest legacy. Today, Americans of all stripes can be proud that the ideals of the founders, though trumped over the centuries by grievous instances of racism and sexism, have finally found us.

A black president can't end black misery; a black president can't be a civil rights leader or primarily a crusader for racial justice. A black president won't stop racism or erase bigotry. A black president is not the president of blacks alone, but the president of the United States. That tricky but not trivial difference suggests that prophets of the people, like Jesse Jackson and Al Sharpton, don't go unemployed when politicians of the race do well.

Barack Obama's journey as a black man has not challenged his claim to national identity. Instead, it has helped to certify his standing as a quintessential American. In becoming president, Obama has integrated the pantheon of figures who have inherited the symbolic role of the nation's father from George Washington. Obama has become a re–Founding Father of sorts, a symbolic patriarch who guards the American way of life and redefines American moral ambition through his speech and action. Obama is now the face of America to the nation and world. It is striking enough that a black man will skirt the irritating limits of race to become the nation's advocate before the world. It is even more striking that in so doing Obama has not interrupted, but rather extended, the democratic ideals of the Founding Fathers.

To see what makes Obama tick, look at his training in the trenches of community organizing. As Ronald Reagan practiced what Vice President George Bush would call "voodoo economics" — supply-side theories wrapped in tax cuts for the wealthy — Obama exited the Ivy League corridors of Columbia University in 1983. After a brief and unsatisfying stint on Wall Street, he headed straight for the 'hood. On the South Side of Chicago, he worked with a church-based group that battled poverty's offspring: crime and high unemployment. Obama rolled up his sleeves — something he got used to doing to satisfy his basketball jones on countless asphalt courts — and applied elbow grease and hard thinking to the persistent ills of the poor. Practical efforts to help the beleaguered are good training for leaders of the free world. The poignant memory of the most afflicted stands a better chance to replay in their minds.

It is supremely ironic, perhaps even tragic, that a man like O. J. Simpson, accused of murder with an extraordinary amount of evidence amassed against him, could receive the black benefit of doubt, and yet in some quarters, Obama couldn't pass the smell test.

Black folk had every right to ask if Obama would betray them, to see if he was more Clarence Thomas than Martin Luther King. And they have a right to be nervous about all the talk about postracial identity, knowing full well that such a possibility is not only relatively slim, but that it's not a norm that should even be embraced. One need not stop being black in order to be a full citizen of the nation. Bland racial identities are not required to help the nation to a fair and just polity. We should not be postracial — seeking to get beyond the uplifting meanings and edifying registers of blackness. Rather, we should be postracist: moving beyond cultural fascism and vicious narratives of racial privilege and superiority that tear at the fabric of "E Pluribus Unum."

Obama's racial experiences may offer him an edge in the national effort to overcome the poisonous divisions that plague the American soul. His fascinating mix of race and culture shows up in lively fashion — including his love for the upper reaches of Abraham Lincoln's emancipating political vision, as well as his compassion for the black boys and girls stuck on the lowest rung of the ladder of upward mobility. That he is aware of race without being its prisoner — that he is rooted in, but not restricted by, his blackness — challenges orthodoxies and playbooks on all sides of the racial divide. But it may also make him curiously effective in the pledge to overcome our racial malaise and to restore our national kinship.

————

Barack Obama has come closer than any figure in recent history to obeying a direct call of the people to the brutal and bloody fields of political mission. His visionary response to that call gives great hope that he can galvanize our nation with the payoff of his political rhetoric: a true democracy fed by justice, one that balances liberty with responsibility. He may be our best hope to tie together the fraying strands of our political will into a powerful and productive vision of national destiny, one for which Martin Luther King, Jr., hoped and died.

————

Obama, something of a re–Founding Father, now joins the pantheon of white men who have cast a bright light or negative shadow over the nation's political landscape. His interpretation of America's ideals and destiny will enliven the creeds that have shaped the nation's self-image.

————

Perhaps even more than being like the Old Testament leader Joshua, Obama is like his biblical namesake Barak, who is described in the New Testament (along with other judges) as one "who through faith conquered kingdoms, administered justice, and gained what was promised." Obama has a real chance to embody the stable, principled black political leadership that Martin Luther King envisioned. And by administering justice and gaining what has been promised, Obama has an authentic opportunity to fulfill the legacy of King, and of Jesse Jackson too. Because King and Jackson fought bitter battles with ugly forces, Obama can gracefully walk through doors kicked in by King and Jackson. As he walks through those doors, Obama carries the legacy of his people even as he seeks to serve the entire nation. There could hardly be a more fitting tribute to King, and to the people and justice he loved.

The election of Barack Obama symbolizes the resurrection of hope and the restoration of belief in a country that has often failed to treat its black citizens as kin. For millions of blacks abandoned to social neglect and cultural isolation, Obama's words and vision have built a bridge back into the American family. Obama's historic win is the triumphant closing of a circle of possibility begun when former slaves boldly imagined that one of their offspring or kin would one day lead the nation that enslaved their ancestors.

As a black man, I feel indescribable elation and pride to be an American on this day of Obama's election as president. Black folk have told our children a useful lie in the past: they could be anything their minds and talents permitted them to be, even president. Now we can stop lying and start working to make sure that Obama is only the first of many more — presidents, astronauts, governors, senators, theoretical physicists, baseball commissioners, NASCAR drivers, Olympic swimmers, or whatever other pursuit we can dare to imagine.

As Obama made his way in local and national politics, he bravely embodied Du Bois's wish for black folk to develop themselves in the white world without being dissed by their own group. It's not that Obama was seeking to escape his black identity so much as he wanted to leap valiantly past racial limits. Blacks quickly got over their suspicion of Obama's experiment in free black identity. They grew to appreciate how he yearned to crush racial stereotypes and revel in a cosmopolitan American identity that drank from its black roots without being strangled by them.

The psychological advantage of waking up knowing and seeing almost every day the leader of the free world as a member of your own tribe brings pride even to the most cynical critic. Maybe this psychic, internal emotional turmoil that black people struggle against will somehow be lessened by seeing the image of a black man in charge.

As the nation is mired in war and economic depression, Obama believes in America. He proclaims our nation as a land of hope awash in moral excellence and political reinvention, a place where people may dream out loud about impossible ventures and turn them to fact. He is fueled by his own improbable transformation from insecure kid to indomitable political force.

As he took the oath of office to uphold the Constitution and to defend the nation from its enemies, Obama joined a precious short list of men who have shaped the nation's future and direction for good or ill. Obama's efforts have not solved the riddle of race in America. We are not a postracial land, and we have not vanquished racism from our midst. But Barack Obama's election as president has brought us closer to the day when a man can be considered an American even when it is recognized that he is also black.

They called him a Communist, a Socialist, a traitor, and a terrorist, but since January 20, 2009, they have called him President of the United States of America.

MED

chapter 2

Faith and Spirit

In this era of global relations, God may be
outsourcing the pursuit of justice, truth, and
goodness to those who aren't religious but
who are willing to do the work.

Spirituality makes religion behave.

———————

Believers at their best avoid attempts to impose Christianity on the world, a strategy as old as religious establishment and as new as national efforts to manipulate God for political favor. Christians maintain their belief while making arguments for the common good that are subject to criticism and revision because they are neither final nor perfect.

———————

Because the Founding Fathers were not orthodox Christians, the views they held about the role of religion in the republic had more to do with its preservative function in national life and its support of political institutions than its strictly redemptive role as envisioned by partisan believers.

———————

The culture of sexual privilege encouraged within most religious quarters — where ministers, priests, and rabbis expect carnal rewards for spiritual service — must be openly addressed. The doctrine of sin in most religious circles counsels forgiveness in the face of failure because human vulnerability is universal. But that's different from the moral hypocrisy that often haunts these religious circles. While clergy rail against the sexual deviance of rappers, teen mothers, and gays and lesbians, they often fail to confront the rituals of seduction they practice from the pulpit. Bedding women is nearly a sport in some churches.

———————

Jean Paul Sartre led me into atheism as a youth. He lured me with his insistence that human beings should make their own choices in a godless universe where the only design is the one we furnish. Enough with God, I thought, even though I didn't leave the church and insisted on pricking the church's conscience by making arguments against God on God's own turf. To my pastor's credit, he encouraged me to remain in church and to run the course of my atheism. My strident disbelief was dramatically reversed a year later when I was caught in the middle of an armed robbery, and I promised the God I didn't believe in that I would use my mind to serve him if he would let me live. He did, and I have.

———

Faith has a large part to play in the public arena, but only if it will describe its goals in a language that is publicly effective, accompanied by the politics with the best chance to make those goals concrete and relevant.

———

I loved coming to prayer meetings because I got a more intimate sense of belonging to a congregation where, like the bar on the television series *Cheers*, "everybody knows your name." Our church had nearly five thousand members, making it easy to get lost in the shuffle, especially as a poor youth. Prayer meetings provided a glimpse of the church in glorious subtraction. The midweek prayer and praise service, as the Wednesday meetings were officially known, winnowed the faithful from the once-a-week-on-Sunday-morning crowd in most churches, much the way Bible study does. Beyond that, prayer meetings offered a theological ultrasound of a congregation's spiritual health by forming a picture of the hidden organs of faith and prayer that sustain the church body.

———

In this era of global relations, God may be theologically outsourcing the pursuit of justice, truth, and goodness to those who aren't religious but who are willing to do the work.

Water is central to African American culture; it symbolizes freedom, separation and purity, and birth and death, all at the same time. It is important in the religious stories we tell to narrate our identity and destiny. The Red Sea opened up in the Bible to clear a path for escaping Hebrew slaves, but closed and drowned Pharaoh's pursuing army. The angry sea consumed and spit out black bodies during the Middle Passage, a watery grave that provided freedom from the brutal chattel slavery ahead. But water is also the symbol of spiritual redemption, of burying sins and cleansing the soul of moral dirt. "Wade in the Water" is a favorite spiritual, or slave song, one that promises the ebony children of God that "God's gonna trouble the waters."

Our faith can give us the comfort that God walks with us, and will not forsake us. That may seem like small solace in the face of our finitude. But the knowledge that God refuses to let us go ultimately calms the soul in distress. That is the only guarantee we have that the universe that has betrayed us at one turn through the perils of nature will stand behind us through the divine Word.

The black church has been flooded by theological support for material greed that threatens to drown our identification with "the least of these." In the meantime, we have surrendered Micah's prophetic plea to love mercy, do justice, and walk humbly with God. Black pastors and flocks must refocus on their mission to the downtrodden, the heavy laden, the socially outcast, the bereaved, and those imprisoned by hopelessness and despair. Too many black churches have failed to translate the gospel into concrete demands for social justice. Instead, we have tailored our theologies to fit the market. And we have surrendered moral ground to a conservative culture that resists our history and our best traditions.

The real wall of separation most grievous to American Christianity is not between church and state; it remains the wall between black and white.

There is a relentless procession, circulation, and movement of black bodies in the black church: the choir gliding in and grooving to the rhythmic sweep of a grinding gospel number; members marching aisle by aisle to plop a portion of their earnings in the collection plate; women sashaying to the podium to deliver the announcements; kids huddling around the teacher for the children's morning message; the faithful standing at service's start to tell how good the Lord's been to them this week; the convicted leaping to their feet to punctuate a preacher's point in spiritual relief or guilt; the deliberate saunter to the altar of the "whosoever wills" to pray for the sick and bereaved, and for themselves; the white-haired, worldly-wise deacon bowing down at this seat to thank God that he was spared from death, that "the walls of my room were not the walls of my grave," his bed "sheet was not my winding sheet," and his bed was not "my cooling board"; the church mother shaking with controlled chaos as the Holy Ghost rips straight through her vocal chords down to her abdomen; the soloist's hands gesturing grandly as she bends each note into a rung on Jacob's ladder to carry the congregation "higher and higher"; the ushers' martial precision as they gracefully guide guests to a spot where they might get a glimpse of glory; and the choir director calling for pianissimo with a guileless "shhhh" with one hand as the other directs the appointed soprano to bathe the congregation in her honey-sweet "ha-lay-loo-yuh."

When the divine intersects human identity, a transforming energy is unleashed that redeems time and gives human beings unshakable purpose.

When Jesus came to earth, it spotlighted a God who, when it came to battling impossible odds, had been there and done that. Because black Christians passed through the "valley of the shadow of death," they took solace from a God who had faced the same ills they faced. Divine abandonment. Cruel cursing. Ethnic bigotry. Religious marginalization. Unjust punishment. Spiteful epithets. And most important, vicious death. Just knowing that God had walked these same roads, eaten this same food, tasted this same disappointment, experienced this same rejection, fought this same self-doubt, endured this same betrayal, felt this same isolation, encountered this same opposition, and overcome this same pain often made the difference between black folk living and dying.

A great source of hope to black Christians is the belief that God identifies with our condition as the underdog. That's why the stories of Christ's birth in the gospels are carefully read and heavily leaned on: they express the fact that God sides with the homeless, the oppressed, those besieged by the state, those who are the victims of political terror. When God was born in a manger as Jesus, it showed just how far God was willing to go to prove to humanity that God loves us.

––––––––

Vital, living traditions leave space for people to change bad habits because they have a better understanding of what the tradition should mean. As one wise churchman put it: *tradition* is the living faith of dead people, while the *traditional* is the dead faith of living people. Too often, the latter has ruled our churches. While we may share our forbears' faith, we can certainly leave aspects of their theologies behind.

––––––––

There is a profound kinship between spirituality and sexuality. Great mystics figured that out a long time ago. Black Christians are reluctant to admit the connection because our theologies of sexuality are captive to the mind-body split thought up by philosopher Descartes. Except it is translated as the split between body and soul. Black Christian sexuality is subject to the sort of segregation we sought to escape in the social realm. The body and soul in worship are kept one place while the body and soul in heat are kept elsewhere. That's ironic because, as critic Michael Ventura has argued, black culture, especially black music, has healed, indeed transcended, the split between mind and body inherited from Descartes and certain forms of Christian theology. Segments of secular black culture have explored the intimate bond of sexuality and spirituality. The black church has given a great deal to black culture, including the style and passion of much of black pop music. It is time the church accept a gift in return: the union of body and soul.

Their faith has long provided black folk safe harbor in ugly storms and disasters, both natural and man-made. When Africans were torn from their mother soil and forced into bondage in the New World, millions of lives were lost on the angry seas. Still, even as their brothers and sisters perished, their faith allowed many Africans to preserve life and limb and to symbolically book passage on the "Ol' Ship of Zion." When blacks were plunged beneath the harsh waves of chattel slavery, they sought refuge in the community of faith they carved out of their brutal existence. When the civil rights movement was drenched with the foul spray of white supremacy and Jim Crow, it took cover in sanctuaries across the land.

On every first Sunday of the month, or whenever they celebrated the Lord's Supper, black Christians broke bread and drank wine, knowing that Jesus' crucified body was their crucified body, and that Jesus' resurrected body could be theirs as well. Every time the words of Holy Communion were repeated, "this do in remembrance of me," black Christians remembered those lost warriors who once fought mightily against oppression but who now slept with the ancestors.

Even as we battle bruising inequalities, we must be careful to resist the Elijah complex, named for the prophet who believed that he was the only righteous person left to spread

God's message and to keep God's people from perishing. But God spoke to Elijah in practical terms that had profound results: "Rest your mind and soul, and get something to eat," God said to Elijah, and I'm paraphrasing here, "and then look and see that there are seven thousand others who have not bowed their knees to the false god Baal." The sense that we are alone, that we have no moral compatriots, is the perennial plague of the prophet. But we are often reminded that God has other warriors, messengers, and prophets who speak the truth. Such a recognition should relieve our stress and challenge our often arrogant assumptions that we are the exclusive bearers of God's word.

Today's prosperity gospel reflects earlier trends in twentieth-century theological materialism, termed the gospel of health and wealth, which emerged in the 1920s, '30s, and '40s. It influenced both white and black preachers. I think one explanation for its revival is the attempt of new members of the upper black middle class to offer theological grounds for their success without feeling guilty, or responsible, for those left behind. As a result, we get a *materialistic,* not a *material,* religion. The former archbishop of Canterbury, William Temple, said that Christianity is the most material religion there is because we address the flesh, we deal with the body. A material religion takes seriously the issues of disease, suffering, pain, death, and so on. But materialistic religion surrenders to an economic interpretation of the faith. It attempts to baptize financial pursuits as the greatest goal of life, spurning our obligations to the poor while remaining silent about the forces that cause economic inequality.

There's this arbitrary sin system that we've established here that says you can't do this and you can't do that. Yet we're doing all kinds of stuff that we know is out of bounds and unquestionably "sinful." And if we would be honest about it, we could talk about how complex our real theologies are. Not our written ones, but our lived ones.

———

Let's be honest: for many Christians, the insistence on the virgin birth is just as much a moral matter as a theological one. The same religious folk who beat up on poor single mothers *have* to give Mary a pass. The fact that God chose her to mother God's son makes her different, makes her special. And thus she's spared the brutal condemnation that single poor mothers routinely receive in our culture. But who's to say that God doesn't still choose poor single mothers to deliver another of God's beloved sons or daughters to earth, even if they get here in more conventional fashion?

———

At the root of so much of the fratricide and the genocide in our world is the question of the use or abuse of money and wealth. That's why we should talk about prosperity in the context of God's plan. God is not interested in the unfettered accumulation of wealth for self-aggrandizing purposes, for self-absorbed "me-ism." It's about helping this nation. It's about helping our people. It's about helping all people in need.

———

As strange as it might sound, God has a hard time finding room in our hearts and culture. Most of us who think of ourselves as Christians feel that we're full of God. We pray and politic in God's name; we bless and curse folk in God's name.

We preach and posture in God's name. And we think we'd never turn God away. We see ourselves with open arms welcoming God into every nook and cranny of our existence. But the story of Christmas reminds us that it's the very folk who think we're in with God who keep God outside — of our identities, our institutions, and our history.

If God is going to be God, you've got to get rid of your other gods. And sometimes God does a jack move on your gods, just rips them off; just uses your enemies to take them away from you. I know we don't like that, but to paraphrase the great preacher Paul Sherer, "Real worship is bringing the gods we've made to bow down to the God who made us." But what do we do? We attempt to make God bow down before our gods.

The story of Jesus' birth — the struggles of his parents, and the tough and dramatic circumstances in which he was conceived and delivered — may as well have been ripped from the pages of faith and dropped right into today's social science textbooks. There's been a great deal of hand wringing and moralizing about the poor: They don't try hard enough to get education. They wear their victim status like a badge of honor. They're hopelessly dependent upon government paychecks. They have too many babies out of wedlock. They don't speak with intelligence or eloquence. They spurn moral discipline and are ruled by lust and envy.

Thank God that the biblical account of Jesus' family is free of such harsh judgments of the poor. Joseph and Mary were obviously without means; why else would they have to resort to a manger because there was no room for them in an inn? And yet the Bible doesn't condemn them for their condition.

Instead, the story unfolds in simple eloquence to suggest their purity of heart — that is, their singleness of purpose — even as it captures their struggles for divine direction. They were sure the finger of God had written in their lives; they were simply trying to figure out what it all meant. They knew it revolved around the special child Mary would bring into the world, but they wrestled with inner visions and heavenly warnings to discern his lofty destiny.

————————

Martin Luther King, Jr., didn't want to create a Christian nation. He used his Christian beliefs to create a *just* nation.

————————

We should offer the same sort of guidance to poor single mothers that Mary got — from God, the angels, religious stories, and human beings. Maybe then their children will be able to prosper like Jesus did. We should hope this is the case for minority mothers who, like Mary, witness decrees sent out to harm their children. Of course these need not be as explicit as Herod's edict to find and kill Jesus because of the threat he posed. There are some political figures who detect in black children's birth to poor mothers a threat to their conservative beliefs. The threats are sometimes expressed as moral fears concealed in political terms — such as the need to reform poor families harmed by "social pathologies" and welfare dependency.

On occasion, the potential threat of black children to conservative philosophies barrels over the top. That happened when former education secretary Bill Bennett pondered aloud the social benefits of the abortion of black babies. And there is a great deal of harm for black children in political and cultural edicts to build more prisons to warehouse young black boys, or to shut schools in poor neighborhoods, thus making black youth even more socially isolated and vulnerable. These different disguises worn by political figures invested in black social control makes them little more than Herod in drag.

───────

We have to be very careful about talking about how God blesses us — even in our theology when it says, "I was spared." I was supposed to be at the World Trade Center doing a book signing the day it went down. I was instead in Boston that Monday night; I could've been on that plane Tuesday morning. Some of my friends and family said, "God blessed you." And I said, "Yeah, hold on, I *am* blessed by God, but not because I was spared." What kind of theology is that? So the people who went down to their deaths were not blessed? Blessing is not determined by possession of material wealth or even by your life. Blessing is determined by your relationship with God. Blessing is determined by your consciousness to know you need God. Blessing is determined by your intimate contact with the Almighty.

───────

It cannot be denied that religion pervades the terrorism — and our response to it — that crumbled the World Trade Center and our national security. When a Koran was found among the effects left behind in a car rented by two suspects in the World Trade Center debacle, religious stereotypes immediately flashed. Many in the West believe that Islam encourages fanaticism and a hatred of our way of life. In truth, the Muslim faith at best preaches peace and human solidarity. As with any religion, the culture in which it takes root will inevitably influence its expression. In countries where Islamic belief has thrived, including many Arab nations, desperate

poverty and the perception that American imperialism has crippled Middle Eastern stability has certainly fueled nationalist sentiment. It has also fed anti-American attitudes and destructive violence by religiously inspired groups.

————

The use of violence in the name of religion is not unique to Islam. Christianity and Judaism are filled with members claiming God inspired their terror. In fact, the most visible expression of any religion, especially to outsiders, is usually its fundamentalist branch. The true believer of any faith willing to kill for religious principles is a blight, whether in Oklahoma or Afghanistan. The terror unleashed in the attacks on the World Trade Center and the Pentagon is not an indictment of belief, but believers. The twisted interpretation of religion cannot be allowed to smear spiritual traditions that sustain us.

Millions of citizens here and around the globe turn immediately to their faith to shield them when terror erupts. When the 9/11 terrorists struck, mosques, temples, synagogues, ashrams, churches, and cathedrals were packed. Bishops, imams, rabbis, shamans, priests, and ministers read from Holy Scriptures and helped believers address the unspeakable depravity they had witnessed. Sometimes, the best defense against terror is a religiously inspired critique of zealous pride and nationalist sentiment.

————

There's no question that former president George W. Bush's evangelical Protestantism greatly influenced his understanding of foreign and domestic policy. I think he felt a sense of divine calling to make sure that all of the values that we have as Americans would be protected. There appeared to be col-

lusion between ideology and theology: Bush's faith had been profoundly informed by a sense of missionary zeal to support the American empire.

We often mistakenly blur the history of American religion and American empire. If you take a close look at Thomas Jefferson and Benjamin Franklin, these are not Christians in the same sense as George W. Bush. He believed in divine revelation; they believed in practical moral guidance. This is not a Christian nation in the sense that people think. The Founding Fathers were not promoting Christianity to evangelize the culture. Benjamin Franklin said, and I'm paraphrasing, "Whatever religion exists is great if it is good for the nation because it brings us together and creates a kind of political consensus for us to be able to do our business." He was not promoting a particular version of Christianity. And by the time Thomas Jefferson cut and pasted what he believed should be extracted, and what should remain, from the scriptures — Jefferson slashed the miracles and mystery of the Bible and reduced it to reasonable propositions — most evangelical Christians would have been appalled. They wouldn't even recognize their Bible afterwards. So we've been hoodwinked by some religious folk to believe that this is a Christian nation, when it simply is not.

You can't be an effective prophet if you're on Pharaoh's payroll.

The Founding Founders for the most part believed in mechanistic deism. That means they believed God wound the

world up like a machine and now it's operating on its own energy. God kicked it off but God doesn't get in on our side. None of that, "We want to thank Jesus for helping Notre Dame to win this football game; we want to thank God for being on our side of the war versus those evil people." Many of the Founding Fathers did not even believe in the kind of personal God involved in human history, at least not the way believers claim today. So, just as a matter of historical emphasis, many conservative Christians have snookered the rest of us. For those believers who do subscribe to the belief that God operates in human history, there are many other thinkers who provide alternative theological and political arguments. People like Martin Luther King, Jr., offered us a language of civil disobedience and civil rights that was available to *all* people, whether you were Jewish or Christian or Muslim.

There are many progressive evangelicals who challenge the powers-that-be, and who warn against identifying the Kingdom of God with the social or political order, or the state, including America. This notion that America is God's chosen nation is not only politically harmful, but it's theologically suspicious. Such a claim involves the sin of ideological exhaustion, as if one form of state completely captures the will of God. Unfortunately, the more cautious and critical voices just don't get heard as much as the shrill right-wing voices in our society.

There is a religious dimension to the black community's taboo on seeking therapy and strengthening our mental health. "All you need is Jesus," they'll say, or "Just pray to Allah." I like to Dysonize the story of Jesus coming down from the Mountain of Transfiguration, where he was met by some of his disciples who were stumped by their failure to deliver a poor soul from his spiritual affliction. "Lord, why couldn't we cast out this demon?" they asked Jesus. And Jesus said, "Oh, this kind comes out only by prayer and fasting." And I like to add, "And Prozac." I tell folk, "Naw, you need to send that Negro to the psychiatrist. Jesus gave you enough sense to understand that — and blessed the therapist with some healing advice." For too many of our folk — and let's not lie, in the broader culture as well — therapy means that you're weak, or that you're not sufficiently spiritual. The hurtful myth that religion alone will sustain you has kept many a brother from tapping into alternate forms of help — like self-examination in therapy — that might be able to keep him sane in a culture and country not designed to do that.

———

What you often get with the gospel of health and wealth is that ordinary believers, especially those who are poor because of structural inequality and social injustice, think that there's something wrong with them. They think that the moral defect lies in their failure to believe or behave correctly, and not in flawed public policies or political systems. This gospel of health and wealth is, in a sense, a playing out of one of Elisabeth Kübler-Ross's stages of death and dying, where you bargain with God before you accept death. Materialistic theology is almost like that; it's the attempt to deal with the dark night of the soul that can result from material deprivation and financial misery by trying to negotiate with the economic forces of the universe controlled in their view by God. I think the gospel of health and wealth, and theological materialism, is a way of negotiating with God about the economic and material limits of one's life. What happens is that those who get blessed feel that they've somehow been saved from the economic hell to which others have been sent.

In black religious circles, a crucial distinction is made between *knowing about* God and *knowing* God. The former represents a strictly intellectual exercise devoid of faith commitments; the latter is rooted in the faithful assertion of an intellectual and personal relationship with the Supreme Being. The consequence of such a relationship is the *performance of faith,* the *dramatization of devotion,* and the *behaving of belief.* In black religion, there is little substance or benefit to knowing God without doing, or performing, one's knowledge of God.

When we close the Bible, we have neither shut God's mouth nor closed God's mind.

MED

chapter 3

Love and Relationships

In some ways, it might be easier to surrender one's life for a loved one than to do the daily and difficult work of making a relationship work.

We must put aside our beliefs about *women* and honestly encounter the *woman* that stands before us.

Men are often afraid to admit that it's much more than sex keeping us in a relationship. There's a deeper hunger, for which sex is merely a symptom. There's a hunger for joy, a hunger for unconditional affirmation, a hunger, in the end, for love. Men have to stop trading away what we need for the hot rush of what we crave. We've got to pull out of the crotch-notch sweepstakes, and stop measuring by the crude mathematical equation: M = HMWB (manhood equals how many women bedded).

Loving a woman doesn't mean that we surrender our pride as men.

A great deal of the dissension between the sexes draws on a deep mutual distrust of the other's ultimate agenda. The only way to lessen such distrust is through friendship. That means we must focus on the fundamentals: our lover's outlook on life, her approach to problem solving, her spiritual values, her moral vision, her social conscience. That doesn't sound very sexy. But it can make for dynamite sex and blissful erotic communion because sparks fly when both mates are rooted in such security.

Black men and women are in the same bed. Instead of cutting each other's throats, let's rub each other's feet, massage each other's backs, and heal each other's wounds.

Thank God there are some women who hope that their man will be better than his failures, bigger than his weaknesses, and grander than her low expectations of him.

Marcia, I shudder when I think of some of the things I have shared with you, and the vulnerability such sharing entails. But such thoughts are quickly disposed of when I think of the gentleness you have displayed about my doubts, the sensitivity you have shown in the face of my fears, and the unspeakable love you have shown in the face of my weaknesses and failures. And yet you remain my soul's closest companion, and for that I have eternal gratitude.

We have a better sense of who we are in a healthy relationship with another person. We get a chance to see the outlines of our faces, our characters, our souls. We come to be known and loved for our real selves.

I married my twenty-six-year-old actress girlfriend, Terrie, when I was eighteen because I got her pregnant. We were both members of the same church, sang in the same choir, and I thought, had the same kind of love for each other. It was not until two months after our shotgun wedding, when Terrie told me that she didn't love me and should have never married me, that I discovered that she was shooting blanks.

Women need to manage their expectations, especially in the sometimes jarring contrast between the man they were expecting to have versus the one they got.

We make love. God makes babies.

As a teen father I had a wonderful boy who is now a marvelous man. I spent quite a bit of time attending to him. I did much of the night duty. I loved my son and wanted to bond with him. I think many more black men than are given credit love and nurture their children.

Too often we've got it wrong. We think that flying sparks create long-lasting love. But sparks can only ignite what's been stored and accumulated; they cannot store and accumulate.

In the '60s and '70s, interracial marriage, whether intended or not, represented a rejection of racist values and suggested that love was a matter between individuals, not races. Few could miss the heroic gesture of loving across racial lines. Those who did often risked their reputations and social status while enduring cultural stigma. It was apparent that interracial romance couldn't help but be interpreted in political terms.

For a man to get to intimacy, he has to feel safe. It's imperative to communicate that, no matter what he says about his fears and feelings, the relationship can bear it.

———————

No two people are alike, and no two women behave in the same manner. We can't begin our sentences with, "All women . . ." It is better to say, "In my experience, women . . ." It is even better to say, "Women are distinct individuals, and I want to know who you are."

———————

Home should be a no-harm zone, the place where we choose to be known and understood. Our emotional health depends on it.

———————

Women, you need to hold a mirror up and show your man the mask he's hiding behind. Some men don't remember they put the mask on in the first place. You've got to gently insist to your man that it's there, and that it's blocking him from his highest good. You know when he's putting on a front because you feel it. It's like opening the freezer and feeling the air blowing over the ice. You have to help him understand that he's not all there. That he's not only missing in action, he's missing out. Say something like, "I understand that you're going into a hostile environment, but here it's okay for you to let your guard down. The way you're being now is coming between us, and I'd like us to be closer." If you share this truth, and he says, "Great, thank you," or "Let me think about that," you may have some grounds for growth. But if his response is something like: "You're seeing things wrong. This isn't about my mask, this is about your cataracts," then you may have to move on.

In a relationship, we must demand only what we deliver. If we're not willing to give it, we can't expect to get it.

At bottom, black men terrorizing their women and children is an act of *un-kinning*, of violently unmaking the black family and dismantling its binding relations one beaten body at a time.

Healthy people have a high regard for the body. We should not be ashamed of our bodies, but proud that they bind us to our God and our loved ones. Unfortunately, we have often pretended as if the body wasn't there, that it wasn't important to our identity, our celebration of life and our worship of God. This is why we don't teach our children about sex. That's also why we deny that a healthy sexual identity is critical to enjoying our earthly existence. We often repress our sexual identities in an unhealthy fashion. Even God depended on the body to communicate divine love. We are embodied creatures, and we men should do as the Bible says: love our women as we love our bodies. If we appreciate our bodies, we'll appreciate our women's bodies.

The continued preference for lighter sisters among blacks bears witness to psychic wounds that are not completely healed. The poisonous self-hatred that pours freely in the

rejection of dark blackness is painful evidence of our unresolved racial anxieties about our true beauty and self-worth.
Dark black women have often been cast aside and looked
down upon because they embody the most visible connection
to a fertile African heritage whose value remains suspect in
our culture and nation.

———————

Women often say they want a sensitive man, but when her
partner shows his insecurities and fears, women worry that
he may "punk out."

———————

It some ways, it might be easier to surrender one's life for
a loved one than to do the daily and difficult work of making
a relationship work.

———————

Black men are given theological license to affirm our black
women's bodies. We have a holy obligation to acknowledge the
beauty of God's creation in black women's unique shapes,
sizes, and styles. That's good news, because black women, like
black men, have been attacked and exploited since they arrived
on American soil. Their hair is said not to be silky enough,
their lips not thin enough, their noses not slim enough, their
hands not smooth enough, their feet not soft enough, their
waists not trim enough, their skin not light enough, their
breasts not firm enough, their hips not straight enough, their
frames not sleek enough, their eyes not blue enough, their
teeth not white enough, their necks not long enough, and their
behinds not small enough. But for God — and for us black
men and lots of other men too — they're all just right.

———————

We must tenderly encourage each other to develop strengths, prune weaknesses, discipline reckless urges and harness raw, untapped energy and talent.

———

We should love black women's skin, in whatever shade it comes, from vanilla vitality to chocolate charm, from mocha mist to espresso elegance, from beige bliss to almond effect, from tan tint to blue blaze, and from cream comfort to black beatitude. We should love black women's noses — broad or pointed, snub or extended, fine-lined or bluntly drawn. We should love their eyes — black, brown, hazel, green, or blue — and their lips, whether pouting, pursing, protruding, huge, small, voluptuous, streamlined, or luscious. We should love their feet — long toes or short, painted nails or nude, and whether they are broad, flat and thick, or thin, fleshy, and narrow. We should love their breasts — whether tiny or enormous, whether sagging or taut, and whether they fit into A or D cups. We should love their hands — manicured or untouched, long fingers or short pointers, and acrylic nails or natural. We should love their faces — made-up and plain ones, oval-shaped and banana-like, ellipses and concaves, high foreheads and low brows, and fleshy ones and tight ones. We should love their legs — long, lean legs and thick, short legs, shapely legs and skinny legs, and legs that are clean-shaven and legs with hair. We should love their hair — natural, dreaded, locked, kinky, nappy, permed, curly, straight, silky, jagged, or wiry.

———

Many women can justifiably sue us men for nonsupport in the court of emotions.

———

Nobody gets a free ride. Each of us must pay the toll and be responsible for our relationships.

We learn who we are through our interaction with other human beings. But unless we have a secure enough sense of ourselves it's hard to absorb these lessons without hostility or resentment. And that sense of personal identity comes when we wrestle with our true selves. If we've hurt ourselves with our lack of self-awareness, we've also hurt the women in our lives by failing to take the risk of telling them the truth. Without truth-telling there will be little trust and a great deal of manipulation. The more honest we are with our women, the less inclined any of us will be to twist, cajole, spin, or strong-arm each other. To have healthy relationships, we've got to be honest about our fears of commitment, our avoidance of accountability, and our tendency to hug the surface of our feelings in fear of drowning in their depths.

A demanding love doesn't mean that she cooks for me because I cook for her, or that I stitch her hems like she stitches mine. She may not be able to cook. I may not be able to sew. Demanding love is not a demand for similar gifts. It is a demand for a similar willingness to share one's gifts.

For a black man to reach beneath his class station to embrace a black woman reinforces the status quo: as breadwinner, he can provide for his family, and thus remain "head of the house." For a black woman to behave similarly upsets the status quo: if she makes more money and is better educated than her partner, the resentment of her man can become burdensome, sometimes abusive. I know a lot of brothers who felt they could take a woman making more money than them, but once the reality of her higher status set in, it usually took on social meanings beyond a paycheck. Issues of control inevitably arose, and the question of who was in charge followed in its wake. Since black men struggle with a society that sets up expectations for appropriate masculine behavior — take care of one's family, be gainfully employed, be a financial success — and then undermines their attainment, black women are often the psychological scapegoat of our anger. The rise in black male domestic violence is poignant testimony to such tensions in the black home.

————

There's no hard-and-fast definition of what it means to be a real man. We're figuring it out as we go.

————

If you're lying to yourself about your most intimate relationship, you're lying in your relationship to God.

————

Control is an illusion. Some days the woman's going to have more influence; at other times, the man will. We must be willing to concede that our mates have strengths we don't have and shape the relationship around what works best. Keep it dynamic — not controlled — and then watch how it grows and evolves.

————

I believe that our best selves are nurtured in an environment of expectation. Love, after all, has to do with acceptable requirements and reasonable demands.

We're living in a culture of complaint. Too many of us men choose to air disagreements and diatribes about our mates in a ritual of same-sex bonding, creating and exacerbating the very conditions we try to avoid. That kind of talk brings us closer to the men we're commiserating *with*, but not the women we're complaining *about*. If we're just letting off steam and then going home less stressed, it's one thing; if we use our dissatisfaction to short-circuit closeness, it's another.

Intimacy demands discipline — an open, honest vulnerability that is maintained while in close proximity to the beloved. A lot of men are scared of the nearness. We pour the fear into our raw sexuality. Hit it, then quit it. We have so many "commitmentphobes" because we don't want to have that vulnerability uncovered.

A relationship is going to have much greater potential to go the distance if the foundation is created by two people who have the courage to lay themselves bare. Dropping our cover encourages our women to drop theirs. Then our erotic joy and sexual passion will increase immensely. And the pride of our manhood, as Teddy Pendergrass once sang, will be in turning "burdens into a song."

The statistics reinforce the gloomy outlook for black women. In essence, black women are less likely than other women to marry in the first place, more likely to divorce, and less likely to remarry. Only fifty percent of black women are expected to be married by the age of twenty-eight, compared to eighty percent of white women. Black women are less likely to remarry after a divorce than white women. Only thirty-two percent of black women remarry within five years of divorce, while fifty-four percent of white women, and forty-four percent of Latino women, get married again. As if to underscore how tight and complicated relationships are for black folk, even when marriages are broken, they don't necessarily lead to divorce. Many sisters experience a marital breakup without having their relationships legally terminated. Just sixty-seven percent of black women who were separated from their husbands were divorced three years later. Although this statistic might be interpreted as thirty-three percent of black women try to work out their relationships during separation, it is just as likely that the high percentage of sisters who don't terminate their relationships suggests an inclination — perhaps the desperation — to hold on as long as possible.

If black men are in prison and not in college, they have two strikes against them in their bid to become viable partners to black women. Black male imprisonment has a double-whammy effect on black women finding mates among their male peers: it separates black men from society, and it severely erodes their prospects for higher education.

Many college-educated black women marry black men with significantly lower levels of education. In marriages where black women have a college degree, only 45.9 percent of their husbands also have a college degree. More than one quarter of black women who have a college degree are married to men who have never gone to college. And 4 percent of black women with a college degree are married to black men who didn't graduate from high school. By comparison, nearly 70 percent of white women with a college degree married men who also had a college degree, and only 12 percent of white women with a college degree married men who never went to college. While black women may prefer mates who are educationally compatible, they have often chosen mates whose lower achievement makes their marriages vulnerable to divorce and spousal abuse.

———

The preference for light-skinned women finds painful precedent in black culture. It dates back to slavery when the lightest blacks — whose skin color was often the result of rape by white slave masters — were favored over their darker kin because they were closer in color and appearance to dominant society. Unfortunately, despite the challenge to the mythology of inherently superior white standards of beauty, there persists in black life the belief that light is preferable to dark. Music videos have historically presented light-skinned black women, or mixed or nonblack women, as the most desirable women. Even as browner women have recently become more visible within our race — a few of them, like Carla Campbell, Angela Basset, and Valerie Morris appear in videos, film, and on television news, respectively — there is an undeniable subordination of darker-skinned black women to lighter sisters in everyday life.

———

Hair has long been for black American women a sore spot — often quite literally when you consider the lengths black women go to embrace or conquer their "nappy" hair, whether through relaxers, weaves, or extensions. Black women's hair is among the most vulnerable features of their bodies because it embodies visible differences that are used to distinguish their beauty, or its absence, from that of nonblack women. Black women experience intense anxiety in deciding to either straighten their hair, or to plait, braid, or lock it in dreads. Black people have psychologically absorbed this toxic self-hatred by scorning black women who wear a natural hairstyle. But when black women comb through their contradictions there's usually no mirror in white America to capture their struggles.

Black culture — by its deficits and defeats and by its defensive actions to protect its interests and assure its survival — has generated pockets of pathology where potential is suspected and snuffed. We murder ambition, slaughter pride. A tortured racial history feeds this learned behavior, sustained now as a self-perpetuating cultural practice. We are skeptical of black folk who don't meet our narrow views of blackness. We are taught to despise and be envious of others who rise and prosper. All of this is different from the routine and healthy criticism in which all groups should engage. I am referring to the pernicious self-doubt, and other-doubt — really, it's race-doubt — that is the residue of collective self-hate. It is a centuries-old reflex borne of pulverizing suspicion of the beauty, integrity, and dignity of blackness. We snuff our children's ambition through despising their intellectual independence and emotional freedom. We target our children with vicious corporal punishment to make them obedient to what we think the Bible says to do to our kids. We beat the hell out of our kids, and when we do, we often beat out their initiative and ambition too. We must be released, and release each other, from such degrading, deadening, deathly practices.

————

When we love black women, we love ourselves, and the God who made us.

MED

chapter 4

Music

James Brown fathered funk; Sly Stone raised it.

When black music is unavoidably appropriated, imitated, and diluted in mainstream culture, black folk are on to something else. With black creative cultures, it's always about *the great next*.

When slaves sang "Green trees are bending / My soul stands a'trembling / Ain't got long to stay here," white plantation owners were being entertained while black slaves were being emancipated. They were signaling each other about when Harriet Tubman was coming through to liberate slaves and lead them along the Underground Railroad to freedom. The double entendre joined emancipation and entertainment in many African and African American musical forms.

That's why the drums were outlawed: they were the language of black emancipation. The drums allowed blacks to facilitate community, to communicate valuable political messages in a percussive tongue.

The sound of America is sweeter, more soulful, and more sorrowful because of black artists. The blues drew from West African rhythms, work songs, chants, and spirituals. In the mid-forties, the country blues migrated north when Muddy Waters boarded a train from Clarksdale, Mississippi, to Chicago, making it the center of urban blues. The music's irony and tragicomedy, and its humor, too, flood the plaintive cries of Howlin' Wolf, the weeping guitar of B. B. King, the salty wails of Koko Taylor, and the artful hawks of the otherwise smooth Bobby Blue Bland — who lifted his signature warble from Rev. C. L. Franklin, one of the great innovators of sacred sound. Their craft testifies to how blues artists ministered to Negroes seeking consolation for the griefs of ghetto existence.

The blues functioned for another generation of blacks much as rap functions for young blacks today: as a source of racial identity, permitting forms of boasting for devalued black men, allowing commentary on personal and social conditions in uncensored language, and fostering the ability to transform hurt and anguish into art and commerce.

Even in its heyday, the blues existed as a secular musical genre in contrast to religious traditions that saw the blues as "devil's music" and the conservative black cultural perspective of the blues as barbaric. These feelings, along with the flow of Southern agrarian musical energies into a more accessible and populist soul music, ensured the shrinking economic and cultural basis for expressing life experience through the blues.

Blues and jazz, rhythm and blues, and soul have all been viewed as indecent, immoral, and corrupting of black youth. To be nostalgic for a time when black music offered a purer aesthetic or a higher moral vision is to hunger for a time in history that simply doesn't exist.

The blues shouts and the field hollers get reemphasized, and rearticulated, in the longing, yearning, feral tones of the trumpet and the cornet. When you hear Louis Armstrong wailing on his trumpet and cornet, when you hear him cutting through the aesthetics of polite society with its measured, rigid, precise tonalities, lashing, as only Armstrong could, in a viciously insistent tone that suggested he was indeed "stomping the blues," you hear the quality I'm talking about. It's anger and joy, anxiety and peace in shuffling cadences that trade hope for despair as he's trading fours in King Oliver's group and later his own.

———

The question of what to do with ragtime, and then blues, jazz, and gospel, was never simply a matter of taste, or should I say, that taste was never simply a matter of musical preference divorced from the prevailing racial context. Syncopation indexed race as surely as black skin. Plus, the caste system was never far away, since these ragtime musicians were not often educated musicians who had absorbed the finer points of European music. Their musical trace had to be washed away from the palette of American music, which was little more than an imitation of the so-called classical forms flowing in from Europe. The kick is that across the waters, European classical musicians and composers were digging this indigenous American music being created by mostly black musicians of a supposedly inferior pedigree. Figures like Debussy and Stravinsky, and even Charles Ives, are being influenced by ragtime, even as the artistic guardians of Western culture are dissing ragtime.

———

There was an Americanization of New Orleans after the Louisiana Purchase in the early 1800s. New Orleans, racially and ethnically speaking, was a mixture of French and Spanish and indigenous American elements. The Creole, or the light-skinned Negro, the French-inflected "mulatto," was the

product of a fusion of black and white. Creoles began to create ragtime and jazz music only after they had interactions
with indigenous Negro or African-inflected musicians in New
Orleans, a fact that causes me to be skeptical about James
Lincoln Collier's argument that jazz is not identifiable as a
black music. One can hear in such denials reverberations of
the stigma of blackness — of black skin and skill, of black
blood, metaphorically speaking, of black styles — that washed
over American culture at the turn of the twentieth century. It's
a stigma that persists to this day, even if, ironically enough,
black popular culture is the idiom, is the grammar, through
which America is globally identified.

———————

Without jazz, American democracy can't swing, can't imagine its improvised destiny.

———————

Piano-based ragtime accentuated percussive features of
black music that were later expanded in ensembles, which
highlighted the shift to multiple instruments in jazz music,
including, say, a saxophone, a trumpet, and a drum, which fa-
cilitated the process of improvisation that was strictly forbidden in classical music, which had to be read note for note off
a sheet. It was eye music versus ear music, music that had to
be read versus music that had to be heard and learned by ear,
the visual versus the aural, so to speak. Since there was initially little sheet music in jazz, at least not to the degree or in
the manner of classical music, musicians were free to impro-
vise, to remake the song as they played it each time. There
was in-built freshness to the music's improvisational quality,
allowing the musicians to enlarge or diminish themes, to re-

arrange musical elements, to alter tempos and tones, as the occasion or mood dictated.

If democracy is what jazz is about, glimpsed in the equal participation of varying elements in the construction of a whole, European classical music is about a kind of oligarchy of aesthetic taste: that is, there is tight control over what can be played, what can be said, what can be articulated, and who gets a chance to play it.

Jazz culture was seductive to white kids, and they turned from the quadrille, the mazurka, the waltz, and the polka of their parents to the slow drag and the hoochie-coochie, while reveling in the blues of the Delta filtering into New Orleans from Mississippi. This explosion of African creativity constituted a veritable Negropolis, a black cosmopolitanism whose influence sprawled beyond its original borders to capture large segments of American society.

In European music you saw the segregation of the body, where the hands were good but not the feet, where the lips were fine but not the eyes, and so on. In jazz, the body was artistically desegregated, freed from the artificial constraints of taste, custom, and tradition. In jazz, the entire body was truly integrated.

The values of jazz include a profound vocal tonality, since the musical instruments were manipulated in varying degrees to sound like the voice. That's why we love Lester Young's and, later, John Coltrane's sound, because the very textures they evoke on the saxophone remind us of the human voice crying, sighing, laughing, speaking and shrieking, complaining, and expressing joy.

———————

Mainstream swing music was the attempt to domesticate the hot beats of ragtime in early jazz into lightly syncopated orchestral riffing. But again, it wasn't Jimmy Lunceford or Count Basie or Duke Ellington who got the biggest advantage from the swing they helped invent. Rather, it was Paul White-man, Guy Lombardo, Woody Herman, the Dorsey Brothers, and Gene Krupa. Harry James, who was Benny Goodman's trumpet player, was routinely favored over Louis Armstrong in jazz polls. What's up with that?

———————

Duke Ellington and Louis Armstrong swung in the main-stream and then swung the mainstream to a black rhythm, and through their music, helped America grasp the need to place culture and craft above color.

———————

Bebop emerged in the mid-forties as Charlie Parker — and after him Dizzy Gillespie, Thelonious Monk, Charlie Chris-tian, Bud Powell, Don Byas, and Ben Webster — experi-mented with chord progressions, faster tempos, higher notes, and more dissonant times. With bebop, jazz went from dance music to an art form to be listened to. Louis Armstrong and Duke Ellington remained jazz's greatest performer and com-poser, respectively; and Ella Fitzgerald and Sarah Vaughn brilliantly explored the American songbook after Billie Holliday's death. Miles and Coltrane rode together from bebop and hardbop to modal jazz. Later, Davis jump-started fusion, while Coltrane pioneered free jazz. Each influenced American musical experimentation while revolutionizing the sound and shape of jazz.

What we now mean when we say American is what we mean when we say jazz.

I think the lyrical depth is what's so compelling about the best of country music, similar to the blues. And just as there is in the blues, there's irony, tragedy, and a sense of humor in the midst of the pathos. All of that is quite appealing to black folk, and we've been involved in country music from the very beginning. If you look at the history and roots of country music, it's deeply influenced by earlier African sources, especially the banjos and the steel guitars. Even today, many Africans on the Continent are deeply involved in country music. They might be listening to Kenny Rogers's *Greatest Hits*. They might be listening to Hank Williams. They might be listening to Merle Haggard. In fact, Merle Haggard might have a bigger demographic in Kenya than he has in Kentucky.

Race shaped the division of music into segregated categories. So, "hillbilly music" was seen as the "redneck" creation of poor whites in the back hills of Kentucky, Georgia, Alabama, and Tennessee. "Race records" were cut from black music. But the division of "hillbilly" versus "race music" reflected the logic of racial separatism — "this belongs to the black folk, this belongs to the white folk." But poor whites

and poor blacks — besides the racial hostilities that raged —
were sometimes eating together and loving together since
they inherited a common vocabulary and menu. While the
blues became identified with black communities, and hillbilly
music became identified with white communities, there was
quite a bit of cultural and racial promiscuity going on between the two.

Gospel's influence is felt deeply in the history of rock, pop,
and soul — in the compressed frenzy of Marion Williams's ec-
statically ejaculated *whoo,* which became Little Richards's un-
mistakable vocal signature; in Alex Bradford's pathos and
understated irony woven into the country blues of Ray
Charles; and in the fiery vocal pirouettes of Clara Ward that
embellished the near-otherworldly artistry of Aretha Franklin
at her soulful crest.

Gospel music initially faced its own barriers within the
church. It was an offspring of blues, jazz, and ragtime music
born in the black Pentecostal churches at the end of the nineteenth century; early religious music consisted of barbershop
quarter harmonies sung a capella by mostly male groups. A
Chicago blues pianist named Thomas A. Dorsey forever
changed black religious music in the 1920s by featuring
women (and later men) singing in a choir tradition backed by
piano accompaniments dipped in a blues base and sweetened
by jazz riffs. Before the belated embrace of gospel music by
mainline black churches in the 1940s, gospel thrived in mostly
lower-class storefront Pentecostal churches, stigmatized as a
sacrilegious mix of secular rhythms and spiritual lyrics.

Traditional gospel greats, including the later Clara Ward, Marion Williams, Roberta Martin, and Inez Andrews, took the exploration of jazz and blues further than previous artists. These artists harnessed the seductive beats of jazz to gospel's vibrant harmonies and percolating rhythms, and transformed the anguished wails of the blues into holy shouts brimming with deferred joy. Performers as varied as Ray Charles, Aretha Franklin, and James Brown started out singing gospel, and the music can be said to have spawned rhythm and blues, soul, and funk. Gospel music gained wide popular acceptance with Clara Ward's appearance at the Newport Jazz Festival in 1957 and with the incomparable Mahalia Jackson's numerous concerts at Carnegie Hall in the late 1950s and early 1960s. Clara Ward, in fact, was criticized in the 1960s for singing gospel music in Las Vegas. Gospel music's real transformation into a popular and contemporary musical art form was quietly effected by Edwin Hawkins's 1969 rhythm-and-blues-influenced arrangement of the traditional Baptist hymn "Oh, Happy Day." The groundbreaking song was captured on a two-track recorder in the basement of a California Pentecostal church and was performed by the North California State Youth Choir, eventually selling more than two million copies.

———

BeBe and CeCe Winans help make visible the implicit sensuality of gospel music, a sometimes embarrassing gift that draws forth the repressed relationship between body and soul. The suggestive ambiguity of their art is expressed in their songs, many of which can be read as signs of romantic love and sensuous delight or as expressions of deep spiritual yearning and fulfillment.

———

Although they hardly get their due, black rock-and-roll artists helped establish the idea of black humanity in a large white fan base. Without Chuck Berry's 1955 "Maybeline" and Little Richard's "Tutti Frutti" the same year, all that came after them, including Elvis, makes no sense.

———

Little Willie John was one of the greatest — some argue, *the* greatest — R&B singers, but few people know his name or work, except as it's drained of its pathos by more famous but less gifted white artists.

———

Jessye Norman and Kathleen Battle — as Marian Anderson and Leontyne Price had done — spice opera with the pathos and charm of the black voice.

———

Motown shaped the musical tastes of millions of Americans with its bright melodies, upbeat lyrics, and crossover ambitions. It wanted to sell the beauty and brilliance of the black voice to white America. Motown broke down many racial barriers with its massive artistic achievements, even as it embodied both the triumphs and troubles of the American dream and capitalism.

———

Nickolas Ashford and Valerie Simpson's elegant, sophisticated arrangements and their literate, inspiring lyrics — which fused the Christian love ethic with an uplifting philosophy of relationships powered by the erotic charge of mutual respect — were the perfect vehicle to spread Marvin Gaye and Tammi Terrell's urban sensuality. These songs also provided an edifying glimpse into the black sexual imagination at a time when the civil rights movement was still waging war for black social and political equality. In their subtle fashion, these songs protested malevolent stereotypes of black relationships while embracing a universal vision of romance. While they made the point that black folk are like all others, they made the equally powerful point that all others can learn and benefit from black love. That's why the songs were both R&B and pop hits; they crossed over to the white mainstream by slipping through the streams of bigotry that poisoned interracial understanding.

Curtis Mayfield defined the gospel-drenched Chicago sound with music of haunting eloquence and lyrics that touched the soul of black struggle.

Along with Sly Stone, Norman Whitfield seized on the wah-wah pedal — which distorts the guitar's sound — as the emblematic tool in the expanding technological repertoire of electrified black music. Stone and Whitfield helped to extend funk modernism — multiple rhythmic patterns that blend frenetic bass lines and turbulent drumbeats in jolts of regulated frenzy. Besides the aesthetic dimensions of funk modernism, which draws on a collage of jazz and blues sounds, its metaphysical heart beats in lyrics that explore black existence. A key form of funk modernism, lyrically speaking, is urban realism; artists probe the complex social and moral properties of black urban identity and the political issues that shape black life.

The black male falsetto came into its own in the gospel music of the early twentieth century, a great deal of which wasn't heard for a long time in mainstream culture. Its pure tones and soaring reach conjured the celestial climes to which it spiritually aspired. When the falsetto migrated beyond the sanctuary, its baptism in the currents of black secular culture meant that a wider range of hearers had access to both its artistic merits and its moral intensity. The falsetto's political meaning was partially derived from its willingness to reach for notes — like reaching for freedoms and privileges — far beyond the pale. Thus, the aesthetic quality of the falsetto mirrored the moral intent of black community: to shirk imposed limits and gain a higher register of achievement.

It is a new world of black erotic hope that Marvin Gaye strains to create through his eerily arching falsetto. In his guttural cries, his hectic moans, his elliptical ejaculations, and his plaintive whispers, Marvin explores the healing and redemptive dimensions of black romantic love. He serves as a voice piece for the millions who identify with his ethical intent: to claim space in the heavens, whether it is social or erotic.

James Brown fathered funk; Sly Stone raised it.

The Isley Brothers damn near reinvented the soul ballad — taking apart its prepackaged sentimentality, rebuilding it from the ground up, and handing it back to us full of honest, edifying emotion in songs like "For the Love of You."

Because he was ten years younger than Jimi Hendrix, Ernie Isley never got the chance to study directly with the guitar wizard, but he soaked up the pyrotechnic vibes Hendrix sent rippling through the homeplace. Still, the shadow of Hendrix's Stratocaster falls mightily on Ernie's majestic craft: the psychedelic, bluesy intensity of Ernie's long, lacerating licks on Isley ballads like 1973's "Summer Breeze"; his atmospheric, weeping phrases that jut just above the melody of mid-tempo grooves; and the dropkick-to-the-chest ferocity of his staccato picks on such up-tempo Isley jams as 1973's "That Lady."

Disco was born in gay bars and homosexual haunts where interracial audiences embraced black dance music. In post-Stonewall gay culture — Stonewall Inn was the New York City gay bar where a 1969 police raid aimed at enforcing laws against same-sex intimate touching lead to rioting and shouts of "Gay Power!" — political activism inspired increased public displays of homoeroticism. Hence the gay bar and dance club became important places to express gay sexuality as both a political and personal gesture. The music found in such places helped to promote the homoerotic ambitions of a gay populace in search of social support and cathartic release. Since whites, blacks, and Latinos mixed much more frequently in gay bars than in most places in American society, the music that moved them was equally eclectic. A new sound matched the erotic intensity and rhythmic ferocity of suppressed longing set free. These settings brought together two styles of early seventies black dance music from which disco drew: polyrhythmic funk pioneered by James Brown and George Clinton, and up-tempo soul music found especially in artists associated with Philadelphia International Records.

The rhythms of funk, soul, and disco stretch the body across erotic dance grooves. Black music moves the erotic action away from the crotch and redistributes it throughout the entire body. Disco promoted the undervalued eroticism of the gay body and the female voice. It was the gay body performing to black rhythms embraced by female voices — of Donna Summers, Gloria Gaynor, Grace Jones, and Diana Ross — that made disco a haven for society's outcast and overlooked members. It also gave disco a social charge that resonated far beyond the boundaries of music. To be sure, the voices of Aretha Franklin, Betty Wright, and Millie Jackson expressed a female sexuality and independence in the early seventies that was virtually absent in other branches of popular music. But the fusion of black rhythms, gay bodies, and female eroticism in disco provided a political lesson in its very existence.

Barry White's heterosexual boudoir bravado and elaborate orchestrations are of a piece with the bohemian rhapsodies spawned in homoerotic fields of play.

Mary J. Blige's art reshapes the blues at the bottom of Aretha Franklin's soul feminism into a brooding female voice of resistance in an age of misogyny. Aretha's generation certainly faced the same forces. But '60s and '70s sexism was cloaked beneath a chivalry and condescension that even black male versions of patriarchy could express. Aretha Franklin's and Mary J. Blige's aesthetic values reflect, in part, the cultural and musical environments that shape their art. What they respond to — norms, practices, behaviors, expectations, ideas — has as great an effect on their art as their particular musical gifts. While soul and hip hop cultures embody virtues to which each musical style responds, the cultures contain vices to which each style reacts.

At its best, pop music presses an anxious ear to American society, amplifying our deepest desires and fears. At times, too, pop music almost unconsciously invites us to listen to ourselves in ways forbidden by cultural debates where complexity is sacrificed for certainty.

The anxiety about what and who is really black in pop music is proportional to just how increasingly difficult it is to know the answer. As multiracial unions of sex and sound proliferate, the "one drop" rule may lose its power. And, as cultural theorists are now proud to announce, race is not merely a matter of biology but an artifice of cultural convention. Such a construction is often used to establish and reinforce the power of one group over another. This view does not mean that black music is solely the product of perception. Nor does it mean that black music's power must be diluted to a generic form. What it does suggest, however, is that the meaning of race, like the art it molds, is always changing.

While black music at its best has often offered a supplementary argument for political change, it is not a substitute for actual politics. And if you don't have a vital political movement, the music can only go so far. It can *help* alter the mindset of the masses; it can *help* create awareness of the need for social change; it can *help* dramatize injustice; and it can *help* articulate the disenchantment of significant segments of the citizenry. But it cannot alone transform social relations and political arrangements. Politically charged music can *reinforce* important social values, but it cannot *establish* them.

MED

chapter 5

Literature, Language, and Learning

Try as we might to quarantine knowledge, it invariably sneezes on us far beyond its imposed limits.

The writer's gift can make us see ourselves and our moral possibilities differently than what our reality suggests.

———————

I didn't set out to be the sort of writer who observes society to change it, which is what social critics do. I suppose, in retrospect, I had two goals: to write like the writers I most admired, those writers my teachers pointed me to, and to write as well as I could about things that mattered most to me. When it comes to writing, even for social critics like me, reading is fundamental. I knew fairly early that I had no talent for writing fiction. Reading it, though, made me feel the hot breath of imagination. I never had to leave the house to leave home; I looked no farther than the page to see the world. I chased whales with Melville. I hugged gulags with Solzhenitsyn. I sank into the tongue of black preaching with James Baldwin. Later, I sprouted wings with Toni Morrison. And I skulked in bleak undergrounds with Fyodor Dostoyevsky.

———————

I was born in language; I was nurtured in a rhetorical womb.

———————

At its best, social criticism is an inside job. The social critic must grasp our frailties even as he urges us to rise above their pull. She must know, like novelists know, that human life is born in story. He must hear with poets the metrics of sorrow and desire. And she must sense with playwrights the futility and ambition that spark a moral tug of war between head and heart.

———————

I tucked Toni Morrison's *Song of Solomon* beneath my arm when me and my pregnant wife were evicted from our apartment — on Christmas Day. I didn't feel completely disrobed or unarmed: Morrison's unblinking engagement with evil helped prepare me for the worst. Her insistence on bending language until it broke the seams of rationality helped me to take refuge in symbols and metaphors. During that celebration of Christ's birth in 1977, something new was born in me: the determination to rise on the wings of language from the ashes of my personal defeat.

———

Knowledge and truth are never divorced from the ends for which they exist.

———

I first quickened to the rhythms of the critical voice when I trudged headlong and ill-equipped into a book about the transcendentalists. I read this volume and others like it outside of my junior high school curriculum. Most of my new discoveries were retrieved from my weekly rummages in used book stores. I supplemented my habit in a daily tryst with the library turnstile inside my ghetto school. There I cornered Jean Paul Sartre and George Santayana. Well, at least I grabbed them by the spines as I swam in their weird and challenging and thrilling words. I strove furiously to subdue their insights beneath my rapidly forming worldview. When I purchased William Barrett's *Irrational Man* and Walter Kaufman's sleekly edited *The Portable Nietzsche*, I slid into existentialism and the philosophical aphorism like a pair of comfortable jeans.

———

I love black language's sensuality, its signifying qualities, its splendid idioms and vernaculars, and its accommodations of high intelligence.

———

I've got no illusion that writing social criticism is the equivalent of walking a picket line or delivering a fiery speech at a protest rally. I've done all three, and each has its place in the order of things. But there is supreme worth in engaging the issues of the day with the help of the intellectual and literary traditions we hold dear, or even the ones we ignore or despise. True, the payoff may not be as immediate as a vote in Congress. And the impact surely won't be as visible as the uplifting actions of full-fledged social reformers like Martin Luther King or Mahatma Gandhi (although both took up writing as social reform by other means), or even part-timers like Henry David Thoreau. That's why the social critic temporarily left Walden Pond and landed in his local jail: to flesh out his view that civil disobedience could help politics find a conscience. Most social critics will not be so lucky, or so brave, to follow the unsteady line that leads from the page to the public arena. But there is great virtue in writing well about the possibilities and obstacles in a democratic culture like ours.

———

The American voice often carries a British accent.

———

Long before I learned what magical realism was, Toni Morrison made me peer into the heart of what couldn't be seen by the naked eye. And years before explanations of her art squiggled beneath the microscopic scrutiny of literary theory,

I caught a glimpse through Morrison's work of how language behaves.

———

Black culture lives and dies by language.

———

I discovered the voice of James Baldwin in 1970, and my life hasn't been the same since. I slept with Baldwin's essays like Coltrane slept with his horn. I fingered in my own imagination the notes the writer played and charted the progression of chords in his symphonic meditation on the American soul. I learned about Baldwin in class, but when I crashed into his searing prose on the page, it was a train-wreck of revelation: about his life, and therefore, mine, as a black male, about our common ghetto roots, and about the desire to sing of suffering and struggle with pitiless precision. I inhaled his first and finest novel, *Go Tell It on the Mountain,* at age eleven, but later, at fourteen, *Notes of a Native Son* grabbed me by the brain and sent me reeling into passionate addictions. I have read that book and all of Baldwin's essays, some of the finest in the English language, too many times, at too many different places in my life — joy and grief, adolescence and adulthood, amateur scribe and professor — to remember when I haven't read him for sanity and salvation.

———

Black women writers have dipped their pens in the blood of ancestors to narrate our tribal griefs and gifts.

———

I met Toni Morrison in 1987 when she visited Princeton to determine if she wanted to teach there. At fifty-six, she still cut a strikingly beautiful figure, making as ferocious an impression in person as her prose made on page. Toni's shock of naturally and intricately braided gray dreadlocks sprang from her head like the mane of a mighty lioness. Her rich golden brown face was centered by a perfectly shaped African nose and anchored by gorgeous lips carved from sweet chocolate hues. Her penetrating eyes fixed in a gaze that was at once cerebral and sensual. Toni was simply sexy, and I saw for myself the appeal that lay behind literary critic Houston Baker's animated testimony to me: at Howard, where Morrison once taught and where Baker was a student, he and his fellow students jockeyed to sit at the front of the class to be near their buxom and brainy instructor.

Poetry made me yearn to warble the idioms that sprang from my heart, but I lacked the skill to clothe them in a language that made others want to sing along.

My fifth grade teacher Mrs. James taught us the majestic cadences of Margaret Walker's "For My People," which I can still hear in the girlish bravado of the two young ladies Mrs. James inspired to learn the poem by heart. I won my first blue-ribbon for public recitation when she encouraged me to speak from memory Paul Laurence Dunbar's vernacular poem "Little Brown Baby." Long before the rise of hip hop, Mrs. James taught me the value of black speech wrung from the diction of common folk.

I want to make the life of the mind sexy for young people.

As a child I loved hearing my aunts talk because of their Southern accents and colloquialisms. Even though my Mama was the youngest of five farm-raised Alabama siblings, she had virtually cleansed her tongue of any traces of her country upbringing. But Aunt Lila Mae and Aunt Mary were deeply twanged. What I loved most was Aunt Lila's uncut, unfettered, thick-as-Alaga-syrup brogue that poured deliciously and slowly out of her mouth. Even when she was angry, she snapped her speech in Southern italics. "Ahsker," she commanded my cousin Oscar, who was a year older, "you *betta* sit yo'self down on that couch and behave like you got some sense, you *heah* me boy?"

When Aunt Lila wasn't around, I cherished visits from my Aunt Mary, who'd moved with my mother's brother Edgar and their three children to Detroit in the mid-'60s. She was always full of good humor. I loved how she got tickled and let roll off her lips, "Boy, *huuush* yo' mouth." Or how she asked me to find the "do-hickey" she was searching for, which, more than likely, was "over yonder." And I loved how Aunt Mary remarked on my love for Gladys Knight, circa 1967, when I watched her on television and talked about her for days afterward. "Ooh, you just be lovin' you up some Ms. Gladys, don't you?" Yes, Ma'am!

———

I read Albert Camus and caught a glimpse of Greek mythology sporting the apparel of Algerian absurdity.

———

The fact that figures like Frederick Douglass and Martin Luther King, Jr., were masters of so-called Standard English doesn't mean that they were not equally in control of Black

English. These men, like all great black rhetoricians, understood the value of "code-switching," or knowing when to speak so-called Standard English and when to speak Black English.

Nobody hates criticism like a critic.

My writing has been pressured, though hopefully not trapped or disfigured, by social forces. That doesn't mean I can't stand at a distance from the events I observe. It means I don't stand at a *dangerous* distance, one clouded by the myth of neutrality or the belief that the critic can remain unscathed by the blisters of human striving.

Black female signifying is a special art that seems to be almost genetically transmitted from one generation to the other. To get the full effect of how black women talk, you've got to "be there" to see the hand gestures, the head movements, the flicks of the wrists, the snaps of the fingers, the shifting of the hips, the turning of the back, the rolling of the eyes, and the like. For instance, you've got to see the black female imitation of Diana Ross and the Supremes' "Stop in the Name of Love" request to "talk to the hand, boyfriend." The gesture suggests that all conversation has stopped, all nonsense has been shelved, and Harry Truman's "the buck stops here" mantra has been reformed in the black female palm placed squarely in your face. And you've got to witness firsthand what is known in the vernacular as the "Z formation": the Zorro-like pantomime created when a sister snaps her fingers three times in the signature style of the masked swordsman,

supplying a black female exclamation point to the ultimate
dis of a verbal opponent or errant mate.

———————

The job of a cultural critic is to examine artistic and moral
effort with enlivened suspicion.

———————

A significant event in my adolescence shaped my quest for
knowledge. I can vividly remember receiving a gift of The
Harvard Classics by a generous neighbor, Mrs. Bennett, when
I was in my early teens. Her husband, a staunch Republican,
had recently died. While first inclined to donate his collection
to a local library, Mrs. Bennett gave them instead to a poor
black boy who couldn't otherwise afford to own them. I was
certainly the only boy on my block, and undoubtedly in my
entire ghetto neighborhood, who simultaneously devoured
Motown's music and Dana's *Two Years Before the Mast*.

———————

Black English is the syntax of black survival; it is the grammar of black self-definition in a white world that attempted
to will it, to write it, into oblivion.

———————

Can we think intelligently about the American essay, that
venerable form of address that felicitously splits the difference
between opinion and art, without the elegiac anger of James
Baldwin and the knowing sophistication of Ralph Ellison?

———————

It's no insult to suggest that most black folk speak Black
English; they do. But we don't speak the stereotypical version

of Black English that is a concoction of dim-witted, mean-spirited hacks. Our language is meant to define our identities and defend our humanity.

Language simply, supremely, reminds us that we exist at all.

When I first read *Invisible Man*, the only novel Ralph Ellison published during his lifetime, the first line cut through my tender teen mind like a sword. He wrote: "I am an invisible man." It sliced me open and helped give shape to the vague, haunting outlines of race that I only barely grasped. I knew immediately that I had been found out by a book that had been written twenty years before it discovered me. I understood intuitively that the invisibility to which Ellison referred had to do with me, a poor black boy in Detroit's desperate ghetto.

If Ellison's first sentence was foundational, his fourth sentence established the summary law of black life in a white world: "I am invisible, understand, simply because people refuse to see me." As I matured, I knew what it meant to live in the shadows, unperceived, unnoticed, an implausible figment of the American imagination. I was fortunate early in my life to find protection in the sort of strong black community that Ellison traces in his eloquent narrative. Their pride in me was my protection. And one of their truest gifts to me was their demand that I cope with my color by fighting back on the page.

As a public intellectual I seek to cast a scholar's eye and a prophet's tongue on the rituals of citizenship and governance.

———

Before I wanted to write the world, I sought to right it.

———

This is what kills me about people. First of all, they tell us
if we don't master the language, we dumb. Then, when we become sophisticated and past masters of it, we abstract. Well,
damn, which one is it? Then when we get *too* common, we're
barbarically folk-driven. Well, how come we can't be everything at the same time? We gonna give out some shrimp and
some chitlins' and some filet mignon and some gravy. You
pick up what you need. If you down with "repristinated mime-
sis," you check that. If you like Derrida and Foucault, you get
that. If you like Socrates and Aristotle, you get that. If you like
"H to the Izz-O, V to the Izz-A / Fa shizzle my nizzle / I used
to dribble down in VA," you get that. Know what I'm saying?

———

Intellectuals have an obligation to be as smart as we can
possibly be, but we have an even greater obligation to be good
with the smarts we possess.

———

I'm down with you on everything you say about the need
for intellectuals to be activists, Rev. [Jesse] Jackson, and take
a lot of heat for it. Don't get me wrong — I'm not saying this
from a position of security. Especially in an academy that
looks down on, and is skeptical about (a), being able to speak
to a broader audience without using jargon or obscure language and (b), is suspicious of the intent to speak to a broad
audience. So you're not talking to somebody who doesn't understand that. And I've been with you in marches plenty of

times. But this is what I'm saying: When I worked at the car wash, I worked the windows. Homeboy say, "You hit them windows?" I say, "Yep, I got 'em." Now I can't also do the front lights, because homeboy in the front got them, and homeboy in the back got the tail pipe; and somebody's got the side doors. Division of labor is critical.

That's like me asking a factory laborer, "How come you ain't at the university teaching?" He'd say, "'Cause my job is to be an arc-welder." And I've been an arc-welder, 'cause I did that before I went to college at twenty-one. All I'm arguing for — I think we're on the same page — is that we can have concerned, committed intellectuals who make the choice to make their gifts available to a broader public. But we must remember this cat here can't do this, but this person over here can do this. "I can write, I can think, I can make sociological analysis. My name is William Julius Wilson. I can write a book that can inform public policy for the next fifteen years. I don't have to march because my books become the fodder for the cannons being fired on the front lines of those who march."

I want to seduce young people into excellence, since they've often been sabotaged by mediocrity.

One of the critiques of intellectuals I often hear is that we're out of touch with "the folk." Well, when I preach and lecture, I'm reaching "the folk." Those critics who say that intellectuals are out of touch have often stereotyped "the folk." Further, they feel free to speak for, and identify with, "the folk," and they feel free to attack intellectuals in the name of "the folk." But I've often discovered that "the folk" — these very souls whom critics seek to protect through claims of our irrelevance — are hungry for intellectual engagement. In the meantime, "the folk" are out-reading, out-thinking, and out-intellectualizing the very people who defensively and condescendingly argue in their name that they won't get what we're doing, won't understand what we're up to, or will be automatically suspicious of our aspirations. I am always in the 'hood, going to the barber shop and the barbecue joint and hanging with "the folk." And not for ethnographic titillation or anthropological voyeurism, but as a legitimate participant in vibrant black folk culture, the kind from which I sprang and in which I feel quite comfortable.

Writing is ultimately about rewriting.

I'm attempting to excel at the height of my profession and at the top of my game, like Michael Jordan. I have no bones about that. I want to represent on that level where people go, "Damn, did you hear what that brother said?" 'Cause I want young people to say it ain't just got to be about sport, it doesn't just have to be about some athletic achievement — as great as that may be — or about Oprah or Bill Cosby, as great and ingenious as they are at what they do. I want young people to say the same thing about intellectual engagement. I want them to have a desire to deploy a variety of jargons, grammars, rhetorics, languages, and vocabularies to articulate views in defense of African American or marginalized identities, as I attempt to do. I want young people to say, as the folk in the '60s and '70s used to say, "Got to be mo' careful 'bout myself," in admiration of such linguistic and intellectual skill. Not for show, but for war — against ignorance, misery, and oppression. I want young folk to say, "I wish I could do that. I wish I could be like Mike!"

———————

Try as we might to quarantine knowledge, it invariably sneezes on us far beyond its imposed limits.

———————

Jewish comedy has given us a vocabulary of witticisms, interpretations, philosophies, and character types — think of Penny Marshall and Cindy Williams hop-scotching during the opening credits of Laverne and Shirley, chanting in unison, "schlemiel, schlimazel." Or for that matter, think of all the Yiddish terms deployed by acerbic Jewish comedians, from *schmuck* or *schmo*, to terms we now take for granted, such as *schmaltz, schmear, schmooze,* or *schlock*. And consider all the Yiddish words injected into the American language that derived from that wonderfully hyperactive prefix *schm*, that, when replacing a word's initial consonant or used before the first vowel, gives a sense of gentle, rhyming derision, like fancy, *schmancy*, or dirt, *schmirt*, or money, *schmoney*, and so on, a practice largely popularized by Jewish comedians.

———————

Kenneth Cockrel exerted a significant influence on my understanding and use of language in the service of social resistance and racial emancipation. Cockrel was a Detroit activist who eventually served on Detroit's city council. Had he lived, he would surely have had a serious chance of succeeding Coleman Young as Detroit's mayor. In my adolescence, Cockrel made his reputation by successfully defending three black youth accused of murdering some Detroit policemen in the

early '70s. That celebrated case was a crucial blow in black
Detroiters' war against a repressive police agenda — appro-
priately named STRESS (Stop the Robberies Enjoy Safe
Streets) — that resulted in the killing of several black men. I
was riveted by Cockrel's relentless, high-speed, and bravely
loquacious appearances on television, and by his colorful
quotes in the local newspapers. Cockrel made verbal facility
seductive; he shaped words into weapons to be wielded on behalf of the oppressed. By watching and reading Cockrel's dar-
ing assaults on the racism of elected officials and policemen,
and by listening to his linguistic skill in defending black
interests, I became convinced that race and rhetoric are
indissoluble.

Knowledge exists for a lot more than its own sake.

We were taught by Mrs. James in fifth grade to believe that
the same musical genius that animated Scott Joplin lighted
as well on Stevie Wonder. We saw no essential division between *I Know Why the Caged Bird Sings* and "I Can't Get Next
to You." Thus the postmodern came crashing in on me before
I gained sight of it in Derrida and Foucault.

The belief that "my story" is a reflection of "our story" has
been with us for a while. From Frederick Douglass's to Angela
Davis's stories, the black autobiography is testimony of individual genius and moral purpose. It is also a record of the
race's struggle to achieve shared goals.

Like a good sermon or a well-tailored suit, theory shouldn't show its seams.

———————

Black public intellectuals have a great responsibility: to think clearly, to articulate eloquently, to criticize sharply, to behave humanely, and to raise black folk's and America's vision of what we might achieve if we do away with racism and the vicious forces of black self-defeat taking us down from within.

MED

chapter 6

Sports

Joe Louis captured the genius of American
citizenship and the protest of blacks against
their exclusion from full citizenship in a single
gesture: the punch that sunk German boxer
Max Schmeling at the height of Nazism.

I joked with Kobe that he came to Washington and killed my Wizards by banking in a running 12-foot jumper over All-Star forward Caron Butler with 25 seconds left to clinch a two-point victory. Without missing a beat, he replied, "Yeah, I couldn't drop a bucket in the ocean that night." The amazing thing is he was referring to a game he had played two months ago! True, he had had only scored 5 of 17 goals from the field, but he hit 13 of 14 free throws in scoring 23 points. But I was stunned that, two months after a relatively insignificant game against a lame team, this three-time NBA world champion, reigning MVP of the league, and two-time league scoring champion who dropped 81 points on the Toronto Raptors in 2006, and another 61 in 2009 at Madison Square Garden — the most in that storied arena's history — would even remember how he had performed. That kind of attention to *all* games, and that kind of memory of the areas where he needs to better his performance, and his ready recall of his poorer efforts, not only proves that he is still hungry to win after being in the league for 12 years with 3 championship rings — but it also shows why he's the best player on the globe today, and without question one of the greatest basketball players of all time.

Black sports often acquired a heroic dimension, as viewed in the careers of figures such as Joe Louis, Jackie Robinson, Althea Gibson, Wilma Rudolph, Muhammad Ali, and Arthur Ashe. Black sports heroes transcended the narrow boundaries of athletics and gained importance as icons of cultural excellence; they embodied possibilities of success that were denied to other people of color. But they also captured the obsession with sport as a means to express black style and as a way to pursue social and economic opportunity.

Michael Jordan was perhaps most famous for his alleged "hang time," the uncanny ability to remain suspended in midair longer than other basketball players while executing his stunning array of improvised moves. But Jordan's "hang time" is technically a misnomer and can be more accurately attributed to Jordan's skillful athletic deception, his acrobatic leaping ability, and his intellectual toughness in projecting an aura of uniqueness around his craft than to his defiance of gravity and the laws of physics. No human being, including Michael Jordan, can successfully defy the law of gravity and achieve relatively sustained altitude without the benefit of machines. For basketball players, as Douglas Kirkpatrick has argued, hang time is the velocity and speed with which a player takes off combined with the path the player's center of gravity follows on the way up. At the peak of a player's vertical jump, the velocity and speed is close to, or at, zero; hanging motionless in the air is the work of masterful skill and illusion. Michael Jordan, through the skill and style of his game, only appeared to be hanging in space for more than the one second that human beings are capable of remaining airborne.

Heroism is often tied to sports as individual or team efforts embody certain virtues, skills, and mastery. For example, basketball heroes are celebrated for the virtue of rigorous practice, expert physical skills, and a mastery of craft required for excellent performance in a team sport.

When the mainstream embraced Kobe Bryant, it did so because of his athletic genius, his good looks, his magnetic

smile, his clean image, his easy rapport with the public —
and, as with O. J. Simpson, because of the widely shared belief that he has transcended race, or more to the point, that
he has escaped the stigma of blackness. Let's not forget that
Bryant has been hailed for being the Anti–Allen Iverson, peel-
ing away the thug image glued to the ex-Philadelphia 76ers
corn-rowed, tattooed, and hip-hop loving superstar. In addi-
tion, Bryant is considered a "Renaissance man" because he is
fluent in Italian, even as the more impressive multilingual talent of athletes like Hakeem Olajuwon and Dikembe Mutombo
is discounted because their roots, and the source of their mastery, are African. Like Michael Jordan before him, and Simpson before them both, Bryant made millions by making it safe
for whites to consume blackness.

O. J. Simpson's sleek form and catlike grace as a running
back brought glamour to a brutal sport. Simpson beautifully
combined judgment and intuition. His sixth sense for where
his pursuers were likely to pounce on him allowed him to
chisel arteries of escape around heaving bodies.

The exploits of athletes give them influence beyond the
boundaries of sport. This is hardly natural. After all, why
should athletes receive tons of money and notoriety beyond
the recognition and compensation they earn in sports? The
absurdity of this is masked by the fact that we take for granted
that such things should occur. That's not to say sports don't
teach us valuable lessons about life. Sports are often a powerful training ground for moral excellence. Take the case of
Willis Reed, the injured center for the 1969–1970 New York
Knicks who was not expected to play in the seventh and de-

ciding game for the NBA championship. When Reed emerged
from the locker room, limping but determined to compete,
several virtues were literally embodied: sacrifice of self for the
sake of the larger good; the courage to "play through pain";
and the sort of moral leadership that rallies one's teammates
and lifts their level of expectation and achievement. These
virtues transcend sport. They inspire ordinary people to overcome obstacles in achieving their goals.

Some figures have served as heroic symbols of national
identity. Others have heroically represented achievement
against the artificial restrictions imposed on a group of people. In those cases, a restriction was also placed on competition as an ideal of democratic participation. Joe DiMaggio, of
course, fit the first bill. His fifty-six-game hitting streak in
baseball thrilled America in 1941, a colossal feat of endurance
to which the nation would turn its attention time and again
as our preeminence as a world power began to fade after
World War II. Jackie Robinson fit the second meaning of
heroism. As major league baseball's first black player, Robinson performed gallantly in the face of bitter opposition. His
gifted play paved the way for blacks in his sport and beyond
the bounds of baseball.

Joe Louis captured the genius of American citizenship and
the protest of blacks against their exclusion from full citizenship in a single gesture: the punch that sunk German boxer
Max Schmeling at the height of Nazism. That punch transformed Louis into an American hero. It also revealed the hidden meaning of Louis's heroic art: beating white men in the
ring was a substitute argument for social equality. Louis's

prizefighting was an eloquent plea to play the game of American citizenship by one set of rules.

———————

Muhammad Ali's self-promoting verse and brilliant boxing proved to be sparring matches for his real battle: the defiance of white authority because of his religious beliefs.

———————

When Lee Evans, Larry James, and Ron Freeman finished one, two, and three in the 400 meters race in the 1968 Olympics, it was an enormously important moment in the history of American sport. The myth of black singularity was overcome by the substitute image of black solidarity. Isolated blackness was displaced by cumulative blackness. The lone black athlete striving against the odds — whether Jackie Robinson in baseball, Jesse Owens in track and field, Bill Russell in basketball, Joe Louis in boxing, and so on — was offset by the image of blacks collectively running the field and representing not just themselves or their political interests but America. These black men displayed back pride, athletic achievement, and American identity in one fell swoop.

———————

Dennis Rodman was acknowledged as the most gifted rebounder in the NBA of his day, and one of the greatest rebounders of all time in the NBA. His specialty was unavoidably representative. He was constantly grabbing the ball off the backboard, taking shots that were left over from the failed attempt to score, enhancing the ability of the team to win. His genius on the court was, in précis, a symbolic expression of black masculine identity; it was a major symbol of black masculinity, since black men are constantly "on the rebound," and "rebounding" from some devastating ordeal. Black men are continually taking missed shots off the glass, off the black-board, and feeding them in outlet or bounce passes to some high-flying teammate who is able to score on the opposition. Ordinary and iconic black men are constantly helping American society to rebound from one catastrophe or another and to successfully overcome the opposition in scoring serious points, serious arguments, serious goals.

There was a time when blacks weren't allowed to play professional basketball. When they were relatively early in their tenure in the NBA, in the early 1970s, *Ebony* magazine did an annual article that featured every black player on every team, something unimaginable today. And don't forget that the New York Knickerbockers during this time were called by racist fans the New York "Niggerbockers" because of the presence of Walt Frazier, Earl "The Pearl" Monroe, Willis Reed, Dick "Fall Back Baby" Barnett, and Henry Bibby.

Muhammad Ali's fists and mouth — both in the boxing ring and in the public arena — hammered home black courage. Like Jackie Robinson before him, who broke the color barrier in baseball and integrated American sports, and Michael Jordan after him, whose will to fly raised the bar on athletic style and standards, Ali's physical skill symbolized black humanity.

Athletes like Althea Gibson, Jim Brown, Hank Aaron, and Wilma Rudolph believed that what you did as an individual athlete had racial consequences. They showed a commitment to uplifting African American interests while tying these interests to American goals. They believed that their performance as athletes could somehow broker social acceptance for black people outside of their sport.

––––––––

Patrick Ewing made about $4.5 million for Georgetown in ticket sales, in terms of television, in terms of publicity, in terms of revenue that was generated. But he got something like $48,000 for a scholarship for that school. So the reality is on the college level, where these extraordinary athletes are making millions and millions and, in some cases, collectively, billions of dollars for the public education of American society, they are not rewarded in anywhere near the proportion to which they've invested their own lives and careers — and they often don't even get a good education.

––––––––

During the middle to late 1960s, the events of American society impinged on the consciousness of many black athletes in a way that had not happened before. One thinks of an earlier epoch, for instance, in 1936, when Jesse Owens made his famous run in the Olympics with Hitler in the stands. The opposing elements were clear: white supremacy on the one hand, black athletic genius in the service of democratic ideals on the other. But racial events didn't come to a head the same way they did in the 1960s, including the ongoing civil rights movement, the enormous upheaval of the antiwar movement, the peace movement, the social presence of the so-called hippies and yippies, and the death of Martin Luther King, Jr., in 1968. Many black athletes became more aware of their roles and responsibilities, not only as athletes but also as *African American* athletes.

———

Any black athlete who gains a certain level of prominence in America has attached to him, whether fair or not, the desires of his people. Folks emulate these athletes just because they're athletes. They want to make the basket catch like Willie Mays or, more recently, they want to "be like Mike." In the 1960s, such identification with black athletes was even more intense and important because they were ambassadors for black culture. Like entertainers Duke Ellington and Louis Armstrong from an earlier era, these athletes carried the burden and responsibility of a message to white America: "We are intelligent, we are athletic, we are capable, we are not here to burn your town down or to be offensive, but we are here to exercise our craft. Furthermore, we're bearing the responsibility for all of those millions of other black people who will never get a chance to come to your television or be seen on your large screen, or on your local gridiron or baseball diamond." The more high profile they were, the more demands they faced.

———

Those of us old enough to remember can hardly forget how in a 1978 preseason game, Oakland Raiders football player Jack Tatum, a safety, delivered a vicious blow and broke the neck of New England Patriots wide receiver Darryl Stingley — rendering him a quadriplegic — with no apology, contending at the time that an apology would be an untruthful admission that the hit was dirty. Sure, there's a cerebral side to sports as well. But it can hardly be denied that sports provide vicarious outlets for millions of fans with a visceral and aggressive payoff.

———

Mike Tyson is one of the most brilliant fighters ever to live, and not just brilliant in the ring. He knows the history of the fight game like few other fighters have ever known it — including obscure fights and fighters, stats about how many punches they threw, what kind, and where on the body they placed them. His genius only makes his suffering — and he's openly admitted his struggles with bipolar disease — that much harder to witness.

———————

Well before the 1960s, sports had a prominent function in the culture, especially *baseball,* which was crowned "America's favorite pastime" and enjoyed unparalleled supremacy in capturing the national imagination. The boys of summer ruled from the '20s through the early '60s. But in the late '60s, baseball got a serious challenge from within and outside its borders. If baseball was seen as the quintessential American sport, the unique articulation of American identity, its face changed as integration and immigration brought black and brown ballplayers into the fold. Then too, football began to give baseball a run for its money, and much later basketball supplanted baseball as the nation's most popular sport. And with the heightened visibility of the female athlete, spurred in part by the feminist movement, things were in upheaval in the sports arena and beyond.

———————

Harry Edwards is an extraordinary figure in the history of black athletics over the last thirty years. He was at the time a smart sociologist well versed in the field's theories and jargon about race who also understood the internal dynamics of sport. So he was a perfect bridge figure between those athletes involved in the '68 Olympics and the wider society. He was a

young man himself, not even twenty-five years old, and served
as an instructor in sociology at San Jose State with these
barely eighteen- and nineteen-year-old kids. So he was able
to get closer to them than other older, more estimable figures
in the black community. He understood their worldviews. And
yet at the same time he had his own charisma, his own authority that derived from his considerable knowledge and education. As a result, he was able to spur their consciousness,
and of course he agitated people as well. But remember, Martin Luther King, Jr., was also viewed as an agitator by many
whites and a fair number of blacks. So in the late '60s, Harry
Edwards was an extraordinary, difficult, and flamboyant figure. Now he's on the sidelines of the San Francisco 49ers and
working with other mainstream groups helping them manage
their athletes. So times change and so does our understanding
of the figures that helped to change them.

When some people look at Allen Iverson, they see swagger
and defiance, a thug. For these folks, Iverson is like the notorious rapper Tupac Shakur — only with a jump shot. Others
view Iverson as a surly superstar whose work ethic is de-
plorable. Sure he has heart, they concede, but he has ethical
arrhythmia. When I look at Iverson, I see a young man who
has risen from poverty and suffering to seize the nation's
imagination with his athletic genius. You see, Iverson has
been an underdog for most of his life. As a poor black male
born to a single mother in Virginia, Iverson faced the
prospects all of his number do: mediocre education, desultory
home life, father-deprivation, social stigma as a "bastard," and
incarceration, that virtual rite of passage to black manhood.
He grew up in a home of multigeneration females who show-
ered him with love and outfitted him with mental toughness.

Iverson's mother was fiercely dedicated to her son, teaching him how to survive the mean ghetto streets of his impoverished neighborhood.

As Iverson matured, he developed into a superb athlete and eventually led his football team to the state championship as the star quarterback. He could easily have gone to college on a football scholarship, but his prospects for longevity were greater in the basketball he effortlessly dominated. Let me put my biases on the table: I love Allen Iverson. I love that he has made a career out of capitalizing on a move that symbolizes the strength of a minority group in its economic and cultural ties to the mainstream — the crossover. I love that he has remained true to his kith and kin — especially his mama, whom I love as well — that loved him when he lived in mud, not mansions. I love it that no matter how much money he makes, he remembers to tap his ghetto roots. Iverson has won respect, and in the process, perhaps opened some closed minds — and hopefully a few doors — for kids who might not get an even shake because of aesthetic or racial bigotry.

Hockey has been accepted as a ritual sport of violence for masculinity in American society, so you can go in there and beat each other's brains out and then emerge as a greater hero.

People tend to forget that in 2003, Donovan McNabb, the famed quarterback of the Philadelphia Eagles, was under vicious assault by Rush Limbaugh, who said Mr. McNabb received kudos for his play precisely because he was a black quarterback, and that people were trying to overlook his passing deficiencies and his obvious mediocrity. And a year later

McNabb was one of the highest-rated quarterbacks in the
league, a sure contender for MVP, and had an incredible sea-
son. So I find it interesting that Limbaugh could make those
statements — the conservatives can assault — and a year later,
when empirical evidence contradicts their claims, the conservatives were not called out.

———

Mike Tyson crystallized the contradictions of a sport built
on blood and brutality. His success inside the ring depended
on his ability to harness an outsized fury that beyond the ring
could lead to great mayhem. Tyson's occasional blurring of
the boundaries between his two worlds — symbolized in alle-
gations that he pounded his first wife, actress Robin Givens,
and a rape conviction — bruised a major premise of the
"sweet science" of boxing: that it is civilized violence. Tyson
became for many a sad brute. He was for his critics a beast in
boxer shorts whose primitivism was made a spectacle to be
bought on pay-per-view.

———

Jesse Owens represented an era when athletic prowess
alone was a symbolic gesture and a political act. When he performed with Hitler in the stands and he ran for the United
States, he was racing for democracy against the scourge of
Nazism, for America against Germany.

———

That's why sports are so charged and permanently appealing. They and the athletes who engage them are unavoidably
representative: we dream we can be like them or we live vic-
ariously through them. In the case of the 1968 Olympics black
athletes, the hopes and moral aspirations of millions of op-

pressed people, in America and around the globe, found expression in the raised fists of world champions who refused to lower them for convention, tradition, or fear. Because they raised their fists, a lot of us back home raised our heads in pride and fought even more aggressively and passionately for the things we believed in. That's not simply the sign of a champion; that's the mark of a hero.

I spoke at the NBA rookie camp in 2003 that featured one of the greatest classes of first year players in recent memory, including future superstars LeBron "King" James, Dwayne Wade, Carmelo Anthony and Chris Bosh. I remember meeting James — or more precisely, looking up at him as I shook his hand — and thinking to myself, "This just ain't fair." The guy was 18 years old, yet he was a massive mountain of muscle sculpted into a 6' 8" frame that made him a "beast" by any measure. Even then he looked like a man among boys, and his play since he entered the league has proved that all the hype may not have been enough! To be that fast, that strong, that quick, that young and that good is mind boggling – I mean he can pass like Magic Johnson, shoot like George Gervin, dunk like Michael Jordan and play defense with Kobe Bryant's wily instincts! It's scary to think of what he'll be when he's 30 years old and at his prime. We may have never quite seen the likes of a LeBron prototype in the NBA before.

Say what you will about Charles Barkley, but I love the brother, because he's one of the few sports commentators world-class athletes — he was one of the greatest basketball players we've seen, playing way above his height as a power forward with a fierce determination to compete and he retired in 2000 as one of only four players to collect 20,000 points, 10,000 rebounds and 4,000 assists — who will speak his mind and tell the truth as he sees it. Straight, no chaser. Sure, he's made some mistakes along the way, but he lives his life out loud and in living color for the world to see and learn from, warts and all. He possesses a kind of courage and honesty that is both refreshing and instructive. Too many athletes and celebrities take the money and keep their mouths shut about all sorts of injustices and inequalities that their lesser known brothers and sisters must suffer in relative silence and invisibility. Barkley lays it on the line by shooting straight from the lip!

MED

chapter 7

Icons

Richard Pryor's unruly comic genius spliced rage into social commentary and brought America face-to-face with its darker brother.

Oprah Winfrey is a stunning figure, a woman who best represents our people's magnificent spiritual genius. Oprah's show, and her sparkling, luminous presence in the world, has done more good than a million sermons and acts of Congress. Her will to better the American people by offering an alternative to smut media is remarkable and courageous. Her support for the black poor in this country when it wasn't even popular has been stirring. Her loving embrace of our brothers and sisters in Africa has been nothing short of miraculous. She is the symbol of our will to survival through the word and spirit translated into therapeutic doses of information and transformed moral habits that provide her the most powerful pulpit in the world today. I applaud her sterling and impeccable sense of conscience, and her refusal to do anything to tarnish the black moral treasury and integrity with which she has been endowed. She has proved that white America can listen to a black voice that resonates with pure love and extraordinary compassion for the ordinary human being.

Rosa Parks sat down with dignity so that all black people could stand up with pride.

Bill Cosby almost single-handedly changed how black people are viewed on television. First in the '60s in *I Spy,* with his Alexander Scott character, who replaced buffoonish types with a polymath, with a person who spoke several languages and who was very bright. And then twenty years later, with *The Cosby Show,* he brought into visibility upper-middle-class black people, who were virtually hidden from broader cultural view. It was incredibly important. I think Cosby is one of the great comedic geniuses, not only of our time but in American

history, ranking up there near Mark Twain and Richard Pryor
in terms of his ability to tell stories whose humor brimmed
with moral vision that told on the American character, which
grew from the desire of our nation to understand itself
through humor.

To the world beyond the church, Aretha Franklin's freakish
precocity seemed to emerge fully formed from obscure origins in the Detroit neighborhood where her father, C. L.
Franklin, a noted preacher, brought her up. In fact, it was in
Rev. Franklin's legendary rhetorical womb that Aretha ges-
tated before hatching her monumental talent. As a bronze
gospel wunderkind, Aretha's gift poured out in a theological
prescience so striking that her father, a past master himself
of the far-flung ecstasies and esoteric vibrations of the back
voice, must have felt that a double portion of the Spirit, *his*
spirit, had fallen on his woman-child. One can hear fourteen-
year-old Aretha on her first gospel recording declaring with
unforced believability that she was heading to a place where
she would "Never Grow Old." Like all great artists, Aretha was
not so much speaking to us as speaking for us, at least for the
fortunate phalanx gathered at her father's New Bethel Baptist
Church where the recording took place. In Aretha's mouth,
the gospel standard temporarily dissolved its yearning for a
distant heaven and seized her youthful form to embody its
promise *right now.*

Muhammad Ali was a great jazz performer, because his
movements were like extended riffs on the great themes of
grace, power, and precision. But he was also symbolically important, and the metaphoric value of his craft was hardly lost

on his legions of followers, as he "floated like a butterfly," like a solo jazz melody arching effortlessly above the backdrop of supporting instruments keeping time and pace. Except, of course, Ali was a one-man combo, varying his pitch, and punch, and the velocity and force of his delivery, "stinging like a bee," to razzle-dazzle his opponents and fans, much like Miles Davis as he switched from *Kind of Blue* to *Bitches Brew*. And in his flight, in his mobility, Ali also struck symbolic blows against the demobilization of black culture and the restriction of our unique voices, as did so many great jazz instrumentalists and vocalists, from Satchmo to Prez, from the Duke to Bird, from Lady Day to Sassy. And this is where, perhaps, we can see the relation between jazz and hip-hop, too, at least in Ali's artistry, because when Ali came out with his doggerel disguised as edifying ring rhetoric — "rumble, young man, rumble" and "I'm pretty" and "I shook up the world . . . I'm a bad man" — his braggadocio behavior prefigured rap rhetoric.

Gordon Parks peeked through photographic and, later, cinematic lenses to record the travail and triumph of black life.

Sam Cooke answered the appropriation of black musical styles by reappropriating them through his silky, sometimes saccharine, occasionally raw black pop aesthetic. What racism would restrict, Cooke would reinvent. His forays into pop genres from R&B to jazz, from Tin-Pan Alley to supper-club fare, allowed him to meet the world on his own terms by conceding *and* combating the dictates of race and the market. It was a tricky balancing act, one that led both to transcendent art and musical ephemera. Still, among Cooke's most lasting contributions is that he helped bring the world of black gospel — itself the product of jazz, blues, and rag-time — to pop music, greatly influencing rhythm and blues and giving rise to soul and funk. Even Cooke's trademark melismas — emotionally embellished extensions of a syllable over several notes, especially his thrilling "whoa-o-a-o-o-o-o" — were drawn from a gospel world then little noticed by the mainstream.

Berry Gordy harnessed the musical genius of urban black America. Gordy sought to transform the blueprint of Henry Ford's automobile empire into an ebony musical kingdom. Motown Records Corporation adapted the assembly line as a metaphor for producing hit records. Gordy fixed on elements that made cars and musical careers sleek and appealing: regularity and efficiency of production; mechanical and technical brilliance wed to aesthetic value; the elevation of a system that, with few exceptions, credits the product, not its creators; and an obsessive attention to quality control. In the flawed genius of both Ford and Gordy, the quality of *their* control was paramount.

Richard Pryor's unruly comic genius spliced rage into social commentary and brought America face-to-face with its darker brother.

The Moneta Sleet photo of Coretta Scott King consoling her youngest daughter, Bernice, at her husband's funeral, not only snagged a Pulitzer Prize, but it tugged at the nation's heart. I remember tracing my nine-year-old hand along the photo of her pretty face tilted by grief, sheathed beneath the black netting on her pillbox hat. What dignity, what calm, what courage. I met Coretta Scott King in person, for the first time, more than a quarter-century later when I spoke at Ebenezer Baptist Church, the congregation her husband had co-pastored with his father until his assassination in 1968. Without Coretta Scott King's tireless efforts, her husband's legacy might not have as quickly garnered national, indeed, global acceptance. And without her relentless advocacy, his birthday surely would not have become a national holiday, the first for a person of African descent in our country's history.

On *What's Going On* Marvin Gaye made the logic of black Christian love accessible to millions who may have otherwise dismissed its most ardent believers as parochial or irrelevant or dangerously naïve. He took his tunes to church and baptized them in the swelling currents of love of God and fellow man that washed over him as the son of a Pentecostal preacher. He glossed a hundred theology books and gleaned the gist of a thousand sermons when he tied God's love to love for children and poor people and for the environment and in defense of peace. Parts of Marvin's album were a soulful update of the Negro spirituals, or the sorrow songs of the slave, plumbing the depths of black spiritual resistance to social despair and personal hopelessness. Other parts of his musical homily were drawn from biblical models of grieving for the vulnerable and victimized — for instance, in the book of Lamentations, where the prophet Jeremiah weeps over evil instead of celebrating the destruction of the unrighteous. Marvin's prophetic vision drew on chords of empathy and disappointment, a sign that one has neither given up the music of community nor ignored the discord of one's own shortcomings.

Though basketball is anchored in the metaphoric heart of African American culture, Michael Jordan has paradoxically transcended the negative meanings of race to become an icon of all-American athletic excellence. In Jordan, the black male body, still associated with menace outside of sports and entertainment, was made an object of white desire. And black desire found in Jordan, through his athletic ability, the still almost exclusive entry into wealth and fame. The cultural meanings that Jordan embodied represent a remarkable achievement in American culture. We must not forget that a six-foot-six American of obvious African descent was the dominant presence in a sport which twenty years ago was belittled as a black man's game, unworthy of the massive attention it receives today. He remains a metaphor of mobility to the heights of excellence through genius and hard work.

There's a concept in theology called the "scandal of particularity," meaning when the universal God becomes a particular Jewish guy named Jesus. August Wilson's scandal of particularity is his unyielding attention to the specific details of black life. What it means for black identity to be assaulted, but also elevated. Assaulted by racial oppression, economic misery. But elevated because, in his plays, moral vision is not the property of the elite. There's ethical wisdom in the everyday struggles of black people. August Wilson has no desire to translate this for whites, to give a grammar of explanation or a thesaurus that might illumine. Just put black life there onstage and assume it exists. And yet by doing that, people can tap into it and it can resonate universally, because it dares to be particular.

Michael Jackson represents all that young black men have yearned for: to turn their enormous talent into capital and celebrity that frees them to pursue their lives with all their might. He is one of the great prodigies of world musical history. You'd have to turn to a cat like Mozart for a parallel figure who, at six or seven years old, is already at such an advanced level of mastery of his craft. Jackson's prodigious talent was extremely marketable because he was a chocolate, cherubic-faced boy with an Afro halo; thus, both artistically and aesthetically, he represented the aspirations for authentic black style of a generation that came on the heels of the civil rights/black power movement era. He put an entire generation of urban black people on his vocal chords for a while at such a young age and carried them, symbolically, before hip hop emerged as the vox populi.

Michael Jackson, at his best, with all the changes he's been through — some remarkable, some ugly and tragic — is an example of the willful transformation of the self as an artifact of one's own imagination. I mean, that's a deep thing: Michael Jackson made it apparent that the black self, collectively speaking, is a work of art, an experiment of self-remaking. Michael experimented with his face, and it changed dramatically from an identifiably black visage to a curious racial caricature of Caucasian shade and sculpture. Michael's face was monstrously deconstructed of its African identity; his face became a geography of distorted possibilities, a fleshly region of racial ideals invaded by spooky European features that rendered him ethnically opaque. It might sound clichéd to say so, but Michael Jackson embodies all of the malicious demons of identity that black people struggle with.

Susan Taylor's fiercely articulate and melodic tone captures the rhythms of the black heartland. Her words are often read as the most pristine expression of black spiritual yearning in our nation. Susan Taylor is black Americans' Queen of Inspiration, the perfect embodiment of racial pride and sisterly solidarity in an age when either virtue has been diminished by self-hatred or cultural attack. Under Susan, *Essence* magazine was an especially crucial vehicle to rebut the vicious stereotypes that plague black women. Susan Taylor — a woman of entrancing speech who possesses the regal bearing of our queenliest sisters; a woman whose trademark braids bespeak a profound connection to the continent that birthed her; a woman whose voluptuous lips suggest our sensuous inheritance from lovely foremothers; a woman whose flawless chocolate skin shines with the incandescent glow of African beauty; a woman whose piercing eyes flash the brilliance of wise ancestors full of majestic intelligence and ennobling warmth; and a woman with a radiant smile that delivers light to poor souls captured by the painful night of self-ignorance — has not only *told* the truth. She has *been* the truth, for me, and for millions more.

Johnnie Cochran has been called a modern-day Joe Louis. In part, I can see that. He fought tough legal battles for some of our most beleaguered black brothers: Jim Brown, Todd Bridges, Michael Jackson, and O. J. Rascals all, in their own ways. In representing them, Cochran slugged it out with a justice system that often punishes black men with frightening frequency. Unlike the Brown Bomber, though, Cochran's gifts spilled forth from his golden throat. He was smooth and silky, an orator of great skill whose rhetoric reflected his Baptist roots and his early days as an insurance salesman. He per-

formed the law, dramatizing its arcane rituals of argument
and translating its esoteric dogmas into stirring, poetic declaration. For many blacks Cochran was the law, masterfully
taming the chaos of white contempt camouflaged in legal language and protected by obscure codes and regulations.

The pride so many blacks felt in Cochran's performance
had a lot to do with an ancient injury to black self-esteem that
not even Joe Louis could relieve: the white challenge to black
intelligence and its skillful defense in eloquent black speech.
Among his many racial functions, the black orator lends cre-
dence to claims of black rationality. When black folk in bar-
bershops and beauty salons said of Cochran that "the brother
can talk," what they mean in part is that the brother could
think. Thinking and speaking are linked in many black communities. And neither are abstract reasoning and passionate
discourse often diametrically opposed in such circles. Like all
great black orators, Cochran made style a vehicle for substance.

There are a lot of reasons why Tupac continues to be even
more popular in death than he was in life: his thug-revolu-
tionary-artiste persona that resonates in our occasionally bar-
ren pop artistic epoch; his extraordinary handsomeness and
perfectly sculpted physique that embody his youthfulness and
our vain adoration and envy of it; his diligent martyrdom, one
that he predicted, and thus, in part precipitated, setting him
apart from other fallen stars like Notorious B.I.G., who, despite his lyrics, fought it like the plague; and his translation
of epic religious ideas into secular eulogies and cautionary
tales. But what ultimately makes Tupac a legend is the way
he made the music he made, and the way he made it easy for
others — producers, DJs, and rappers — to make something

of the poetry he left behind. Even that may not satisfactorily explain his enduring appeal. Perhaps it is because he spoke straight from the heart that we recognized that a troubled prophet had risen to articulate a truth that we couldn't possibly live without. While that is certainly not true for all of us, perhaps not even for most of us, it is true for enough of us. For those folk, Tupac's searing voice is a siren of sanity.

Angela Davis's hairstyle in the '70s was a crucial political symbol to a people who had been taught to hate our bodies and appearances. Her Afro was a symbolic salvo in the war to liberate our identities from the worship of the white world, a liberation that was embodied in the "Black Is Beautiful" slogan that many blacks adopted. When Davis's Afro'd image mushroomed across the global mediascape, it did more than highlight the extraordinary attractiveness of a political renegade. Her presence underscored the legitimacy of black attempts to wrest the dignity of our images from the vicious machinery of self-denigration. Moreover, her willingness to sacrifice her freedom in the most dangerous fashion possible made an important statement about how social privilege breeds moral responsibility. Angela Davis's beauty didn't merely reside in her physical stature; it was bone-deep, rooted in the love of black flesh, 'fros, and freedom. When ubiquitous posters of her flooded the ghetto of Detroit, demanding her freedom from political imprisonment in the early '70s, I pointed to them with a profound sense of identification that I didn't fully understand until years later, when my critical instincts caught up with my "natural" impulses.

When I met her in 1992, Myrlie Evers-Williams still ached in the unfulfilled hope to destroy the bigotry that had marred her family's life and the lives of millions of others. She fairly shook with rage at her martyred husband Medgar Evers's killer, who was free to spread his venomous beliefs. Evers-Williams was an open wound of memory. She poured out stories of the fight for justice in what was arguably the most racially menacing state in the nation. I found it refreshing that her passions were palpable, and that her commitment to justice was steady and determined. Her pain was raw. Myrlie's discourse was hot with the blood of remembrance splashed across its sharp edges — it was if Medgar had been murdered yesterday. I admired her spunk, her fire, her war against amnesia, an amnesia that led too many of us to forget that, despite our undeniable progress, we had not yet made it to the Promised Land. Her birth certificate might have made her old school, but her birthright as a daughter of suffering gave her an instant passport into the geography of hurt that was occupied by millions of poor black youth.

At first blush, it may seem that Denzel Washington failed to stand and "represent" when he received his 2002 best actor Oscar at the Academy Awards ceremony. But that would be a severe misreading of the politics of signifying that thread through black culture. Looking up to the balcony where Sidney Poitier sat — having received an honorary Oscar earlier before delivering a stately speech — Washington said, "Forty years I've been chasing Sidney . . ." He joked with Poitier, and the academy, by playfully lamenting his being awarded an Oscar on the same night that his idol was feted. Washington, for a fleeting but telling moment, transformed the arena of his award into an intimate platform of conversation between himself and his progenitor that suggested, "This belongs to us, we are not interlopers, nobody else matters more than we do." Thus, Washington never let us see him sweat, behaving as if it was natural, if delayed, that he should receive the highest recognition of his profession. His style was political in the way that only black cool can be when the stakes are high and its temperature must remain low, sometimes beneath the detection of the powers-that-be that can stamp it out. This is not to be confused with spineless selling out. Nor is it to be seen as yielding to the cowardly imperative to keep one's mouth shut in order to hang on to one's privilege. Rather, it is the strategy of those who break down barriers and allow the chroniclers of their brokenness to note their fall.

Betty Shabazz waged an important war to rescue her husband Malcolm X's reputation from naysayers who claimed he was a divisive symbol of violence and hatred. Betty Shabazz worked indefatigably to rear her six children and to make certain that Malcolm's true legacy was honored. Because Malcolm insisted on blacks loving and learning from themselves before they invited the wider, whiter world into the fold, he was a less obvious choice than Martin Luther King or Medgar Evers to be feted by cultural forces beyond — and at times, within — his community. But Shabazz's efforts helped to underscore the ecumenical and international dimensions of Malcolm's surprisingly catholic racial politics.

Chris Rock is a brilliant comedian who lampoons and satirizes some of the weaknesses he finds in black communities. In his instant classic HBO comedy special, *Bring the Pain*, and in his comedic audio recordings, Rock is a genius in figuring out a middle ground between the vicious assault on black culture and the self-critical practices that are demanded of any serious social commentator. One of the ingenious things that Chris Rock is doing is making white America aware of the contradictions and conflicts within black culture of which they may have been oblivious. In one sense, Rock is a cultural translator, an arbiter of contested black meanings in a safe public space of comedy where he's able to broach controversial issues. Even if we are turned off by what Chris Rock says, it is healthier to have open rather than closed cultural conversations — I suppose it's where Chris Rock meets Karl Popper.

In that sense, I celebrate Chris Rock's transgressive notions of blackness. I think it's crucial, even if it is hurtful and controversial, for Chris Rock to go on television — including his appearance on *Oprah*, a show watched by 20 million people, most of whom are white — and talk with devastating accuracy, as well as some measure of pitiless self-examination, of our culture. That's why I think he's one of the most important African American comedians and critics. His *Bring the Pain* ranks right up there with classic black stand-up comedic performances caught on tape, including Richard Pryor's *Richard Pryor: Live and Smokin'* and *Richard Pryor: Live in Concert*, Bill Cosby's *Bill Cosby: Himself*, and Eddie Murphy's *Delirious* and *Raw*. Whether we agree with him at every turn or not, Chris Rock is a crucial cultural presence, a valuable gadfly, and above all, a great comedian, which I'm sure is his ultimate goal.

Mary Wilson is one-third of the greatest girl group in the history of music, The Supremes. I always had a huge crush on Mary because she was a pretty chocolate doll, an adorable chanteuse with a golden pair of pipes — although she never got full credit for her talent — and a face and figure as comely as her vocal gifts. When I met Mary at fifty-six she was still a chocolate dream, her pretty face radiant and full, her beautiful eyes alive and sparkling, her hair large and lovely, her lips wet and pouty, her figure fetching and eye-grabbing. I also like Mary because she was the group's griot, its truth-teller, and a politically sensitive scribe who penned books, made music, and mounted her own career long after the great Diana Ross flew the coop. I liked it that Mary proved she, too, was great and gritty. Her earthy sensuality and her quick mind were true assets in making her a diva who couldn't be dismissed.

Jean-Michel Basquiat's powerful and disturbing art undercut the notion of a single, or simple, black esthetic.

Vanessa Williams has made a career of reinventing herself. From deposed Miss America to multifaceted recording artist and actress on film, television, and stage, Williams's many successes have made her past troubles seem a necessary step to achievement. Her first two albums imaginatively experimented with dance grooves and brilliantly exploited her inherent sensuality as a performer. This last move was shrewd, even courageous. For starters, Williams successfully transformed and repackaged the sexuality that had drawn derision from her critics when she posed nude. But with the critically celebrated embrace of a sexual self in her music and onscreen, Williams has flouted arbitrary conventions that bring stigma to some artists while leaving others unscathed.

Dick Gregory built on the work of black comics who were among the first to perform before mainstream crowds, including Timmie Rogers, Nipsey Russell, George Kirby, and Slappy White. But his penetrating racial observations catapulted Gregory to greater acclaim and a bigger white audience than any black comic before him. Gregory's influence was at once mythic and smothering. Any young black comic hoping to share even a fraction of Gregory's spotlight would have to shine with the gifts Gregory bequeathed: acerbic attacks on the color line, witty self-mockery, and telling the truth about black life in white America.

———————

As Halle Berry strode to the podium to accept her 2002 best actress Oscar, the first for a black woman, she wept uncontrollably and gasped, "This moment is so much bigger than me." Berry electrified her audience, speaking with intelligence and rousing emotion of how her Oscar was made possible by the legendary likes of Dorothy Dandridge, Lena Horne, and Diahann Carroll. And in a stunning display of sorority in a profession torn by infighting and narcissism, Berry acknowledged the efforts of contemporary black actresses Angela Basset, Jada Pinkett Smith, and Vivica Fox. But it was when Berry moved from ancestors and peers to the future that she spoke directly to her award's symbolic meaning. She gave the millions who watched around the globe not only a sorely needed history lesson but instruction as well in courageously identifying with the masses. Berry tearfully declared that her award was for "every nameless, faceless woman of color" who now has a chance, since "this door has been opened." Black pride couldn't find a more eloquent voice. Berry's courage and candor are depressingly rare among famed blacks with a lot on the line: money, prestige, reputation, and work. Many covet the limelight's payoffs but cower at its demands. Even fewer speak up about the experiences their ordinary brothers and sisters endure — and if they are honest, that they themselves too often confront — on a daily basis. Berry proved that on such occasions, black pride's payoff is the shining and unapologetic representation of the aspirations of ordinary people to do extraordinary deeds.

MED

chapter 8

Justice and Suffering

Justice is what love sounds like

when it speaks in public.

Justice is what love sounds like when it speaks in public.

We have to be willing to wish for every other group what we wish for our own if we are to make the identification of the public good with the good of our group work.

The fact that rappers are struggling with suffering and evil proves that in fact they are connected to a moral tradition that they have seemingly rejected.

The public good is hampered when we idolize our slice of the social welfare and elevate our group above all others in the political order. Such a thing is bad enough if groups simply aspire to unjust social dominance, but if they've got the power to get it done, it greatly harms the commonweal.

In the Bible, in Ezekiel, it says, "I sat where they sat." That's *before* he prophesized to them. That's *before* he opened his mouth. Because when you sit where they sit, you see what they see. And when you see what they see, you hear what they say. And when you hear what they say, after seeing what they see, after sitting where they sit, you know what they know. Ezekiel was a theological observer who was willing to be humble in the face of the data he would collect before he made analysis and prescription about the suffering he witnessed.

If we are to maintain any semblance of fairness, we must bring terrorists before international courts of justice that have proved proficient in prosecuting war criminals from Nuremberg to Bosnia. To do less would be to extend a marred record of American governmental justification of misdeeds in the name of protecting our democracy. The ultimate safeguard against such distortion is to behave justly, even when dealing with the enemies of our country. Otherwise, we are no better than the unprincipled and destructive terrorists we condemn.

If Martin Luther King, Jr., were alive, he would talk about the economic inequality and fundamental social injustice that is ethnically based and racially informed — but also class based, because poor white people themselves have been duped by politicians who don't have their best interests at heart.

I suppose, in retrospect, it would be fair to say that one of the reasons I became an intellectual was to talk back to suffering — and if possible, to relieve it. I wanted to be as smart as I could be about the pain and heartache of people I knew were unjustly oppressed.

Some social scientific research suggests that the out-migration of blacks and Latinos from the postindustrial urban inner cities left these people bereft of role models and moral capital — that is, the ability to act right and behave right. That's why we've got all these terribly isolated families. And I think that's ridiculous. There is a kind of nostalgia that suggests, "Well, back in my day, fifty years ago, when segregation happened, we loved each other, we disciplined each others' kids, and we had a great community." As if there was no economic inequality. As if there were not internal divisions that we have scarcely talked about tonight. So I think we don't have to romanticize the past. But we also have to talk about how we can make equality the principle for these collapsed postindustrial urban centers where people are suffering enormously.

I am now far less interested in saving men's souls from the hell to come as I am in inspiring my listeners to relieve the suffering of victims who live in hell in Detroit or Delhi.

The use of racial profiling, indefensible detentions, and unjust raids only perpetuates the belief that our nation is practicing reverse terrorism. If we are to root out terrorism, we must make certain that our efforts don't negate the very principles to which we claim allegiance: justice, truth, and freedom. If we deploy unjust practices to attain just ends, we not only leave a legally twisted trail of justifications, but we undercut the ethical legs upon which we stand in the resistance to terrorism.

Charity is no substitute for justice.

When Martin Luther King, Jr., and other figures in the 1960s argued for a colorblind society, it was within the context of a struggle — a bitter, colossal struggle — for freedom, equality and justice. And black people in the past have mixed their blood with the soil of American society to defend rights that they could not themselves enjoy at home. And if African American people, and Latino people, and Native American people, and the Vietnamese and Pacific Islanders and whosoever will — these "huddled masses" — have come here seeking opportunity, and have had that opportunity, to a certain degree, extended to them, then we must embrace the American dream as an extension of the democratic project.

If we never challenge a social order that allows some to accumulate wealth — even if they decide to help the less fortunate — while others are shortchanged, then even acts of kindness may end up supporting unjust arrangements.

What guides all of my thought and action is the belief that human beings who think creatively and act boldly can shape history and relieve suffering for the good of the neighborhood and the planet.

We must never ignore the injustices that make charity necessary, or the inequalities that make it possible.

Black politicians very much have to be responsible to the social justice issue. Many of them get up there and get a pass because they are black — because they have black skin doesn't mean they represent black interests. And black interests should not be narrowly defined.

Affirmative action is not about retaliating against white Americans. It is about recognizing the legal and moral consequences of practicing subjugation for well over three hundred years. I wish this was a kind of sitcom, perhaps *Bewitched*, where we could wrinkle our noses and erase memories of racial and ethnic bigotry and brutality. But the reality is that we live in the aftermath, with the consequences, of the systematic exclusion of African Americans and other minorities from the larger circle of American privilege. This is not about the politics of resentment; it is about the politics of justice and equal opportunity. And equal opportunity means we not only have to pay attention to the past, we must pay attention to the present.

It ain't about love. It's about justice. And justice says that "Even if I love you, don't use my love for you to exploit me."

Black people and Jewish people have in common the struggle against oppression and suffering, by means of words, by means of thought, by means of aesthetic expression, and by trying to figure out our place in the world by locating ourselves in relationship to God.

On 9/11, I think America felt for the first time the ugly intensity of black vulnerability. Since black folk have valiantly combated racial terror for so long in this country, the question the nation must ask is whether it will behave like those African American heroes who pressed their righteous cause against a white supremacist government that hurt us. Did we try to blow it up? No. Did we try to subvert the process of justice? No. We created more justice by loving the hell out of our enemies.

If you're a celebrity and you've got face recognition and you've got high visibility, you're just simply going to get a different brand of justice than the average Joe Schmo.

You can't be courageous without having love. You can't love without having compassion. You can't have compassion without seeking justice. You know, as the common rally cry goes forth, no justice, no peace. That signifies that the virtues are unified — you can't really have one without having them all.

Self-help only makes sense when the selves black folk work valiantly to fashion can count on the opportunity and justice their land promises all its citizens.

America has often been incapable of distinguishing its valiant role in opposing injustice on one shore from its vicious role in extending it in other theaters.

Many colors were present in Hurricane Katrina's multicultural stew of suffering, but the dominant color was black. From the sight of it, this was the third world — a misnomer, to be sure, since people of color are two-thirds of the world's population. The suffering on screen created cognitive dissonance; it suggested that this must be somewhere in India, or the outskirts of Biafra. This surely couldn't be the United States of America — and how cruelly that term seemed to mock those poor citizens who felt disunited and disconnected and just plain dissed by their government. This couldn't be the richest and most powerful nation on the globe, leaving behind some of its poorest citizens to fend for themselves.

Former president George Bush's slow response to black suffering by wind and water in Katrina was but a symptom of a larger, equally dangerous political neglect.

Bush's obsession with fighting terror robbed him of the capacity to pay attention to the civil liberties and social justice that, ostensibly, were part of the reasons the troops were in Iraq to begin with.

Charity is episodic and often driven by disaster. We need structures of justice that perpetuate the good will intended in charity. Justice allows charity to live beyond crisis.

Unless we learn to talk about class, poverty, and color, and the distinctive way they merge to deprive people of healthy life chances, we are perpetuating a legacy of injustice.

Until we radically alter our educational system, and solve the problem of poverty and social deprivation, our children will continue to spiral down stairwells of suffering and oppression.

Tupac constantly questioned his direction by filling his lyrics with characters who were both the victims and perpetrators of crime, characters who were thugs begging God for guidance through the minefields of self-destruction, characters leaving the ghetto while others stayed, characters who asked why they suffered even as they imposed suffering. In that haze of morbid contradictions, Tupac shone the light of his dark, brooding, pensive spirit, refusing to close his eyes to the misery he saw, risking everything to bear witness to the pain he pondered and perpetuated. In a word, a show like *The Sopranos* offers, in critic Ernest Becker's term, an "anthropodicy," where we hold each other accountable for the suffering and evil imposed, whereas Tupac wrestles with a theodicy, the effort to square belief in God with the evil that prevails, which is at root an attempt to explain the suffering of those he loved.

Malcolm X was nobly committed to expressing how black people were suffering; he was serious about detailing the nature of the hell blacks endured.

The Harry Potter books have captured the imaginations of youth and adults alike because they speak powerfully to the alienation, stigma, and suffering that children face.

If sleep is the cousin of death, then depression is its little brother.

The deeper Martin Luther King, Jr., sank into a private hell of unquenchable bleakness, the higher he rose in pulpits and rostrums across the nation to preach the fear from his own breast, and those of his fellow strivers. Just as he gave most of his pocketbook and preaching to the movement, King offered up his despondency as well.

Martyrdom forced onto Martin Luther King's dead body the face of a toothless tiger. His threat has been domesticated, his danger sweetened. His depressions and wounds have been turned into waves and smiles. There is little suffering, only light and glory. King's more challenging rhetoric has gone unemployed, left homeless in front of the Lincoln Memorial, blanketed on freezing nights in dream metaphors, feasting on leftovers of hope-lite, drinking discarded cans of diet optimism.

Charity is a hit-or-miss proposition; folk who tire of giving stop doing so when they think they've done enough. Justice seeks to take the distracting and fleeting emotions out of giving. Justice does not depend on feeling to do the right thing. It depends on right action and sound thinking about the most helpful route to the best outcome.

For many conservative Christians, the matter is settled, cut and dried, black and white: sinners suffer, the saved are spared. But for many Christians, and believers of other faiths, the problem of suffering presents a peculiar problem: how one can maintain that God has all the power and goodness in the world and yet allows evil to flourish. In classic theological terms, that is the problem of theodicy, a problem that, after Hurricane Katrina, or a train wreck, or the Iraq war, cries out for an answer. It rushes forth in the question: where was God in this crisis? Like latter-day Jobs, the faithful wrestle with why God allows bad things to happen to good people. For many conservative Christians, bad things mostly happen to bad people.

Suffering is an unavoidable aspect of our human pilgrimage; the deepest faith cannot prevent our walk through the valley of the shadow of death.

Frankenstein was the name of the doctor, not the monster.

In making the familiar argument that God refrains from imposing on us the divine will, and instead permits human action to count, for ill or good, we underscore an odd twist in such a position: that it is God's love for us that allows us to suffer. At first blush, such a reading appears headed toward theological masochism. On second thought, perhaps it is proper to highlight the paradox nonetheless, if for no other reason than to show that God is caught in the same dilemma we are, but from the other side. God shares a frustration, born of love and respect for human freedom, of not being able to derail the machinery of time and circumstance to help us, since that very machinery has at other moments brought such pleasure and profit — from great works of art to splendid human uses of nature's forces.

The suffering that human beings endure is never God's will. The evil that is wrought by human beings and the chaos that is unleashed by nature express neither God's vision nor vengeance, as punitive theologies suggest. God's will is for human beings to flourish and for us to live in harmony with each other and nature.

To assume that New Orleans during Hurricane Katrina was a greater divine target for wiping out poor blacks than bigger cities with bigger black populations is to accuse God of poor sight or planning. And if God wanted to destroy abortion clinics, there are more in other states — say in California or New York — than in Louisiana. Does New Orleans contain more gay folk than Los Angeles? Of course, one supposes by this logic that where wind fails, quaking earth quenches queer desire all the same. But thousands of straight people die in earthquakes, just as they do in hurricanes. Did no conservative Christians die in the flood? Either God's aim is off, or the advocates of divine wrath believe that these innocents are *theolateral* damage. But does God punish the innocent to get a message to the guilty? What about the babies who died, who practiced neither abortion nor voodoo, and who hadn't claimed their sexual orientation or engaged in racial politics? Such a gesture is dirty pool, even for divinity.

We must be willing to be kept awake in another's bed of pain before lashing them for being morally asleep.

MED

chapter 9

Arts

When we lived in a less sophisticated
technological era where we couldn't get music
through a quick download or file sharing over
the Internet, we had to do it the old-fashioned
way: stand before "The Stereo" and place the
stylus over the rotating, compressed wax and
allow the analog vibrations to brush across our
soundscape and through our nearly busted
woofers and tweeters.

Michael Jackson's passage from music superstar to global phenomenon leapt to life on May 16, 1983, with his mythic dance performance of the "moonwalk" on the *Motown 25* television special, which was beamed to almost 50 million viewers around the world. Jackson's skill and imagination came together in immortal movements which captured the genius of street dance, Fred Astaire's agile dance steps, and the creativity of black dancers like Bojangles, Sammy Davis, and Katherine Dunham, who created great art despite huge odds.

The popular dances of the 1920s reflected the influence of space on aesthetics. For instance, in polite society they danced the quadrille, the mazurka, the waltz, and the polka in association with chamber music. But when there were open spaces and markedly vibrant dance halls, all characteristically where "the folk" gathered, the dances were the slow drag, the eagle rock, and the buzzard lope. All in all, the music and dance outside "official" society — and music and dance were intimately connected — reflected the infusion of African aesthetic values by means of New Orleans Creoles.

Hip hop cannot be divorced from its roots in Jamaica. In the 1960s, sound system operators hauled massive speakers in wooden carts in working-class communities during backyard dances attended by "rude boys," the Caribbean counterpart to hip hop's "b-boys." Also, the Jamaican dance hall was the site of a mixture of older and newer forms of Caribbean music, including calypso, soca, salsa, Afro-Cuban, ska, and reggae. One of the first great pioneers of hip hop, DJ Kool Herc, was a West Indian immigrant to the West Bronx who brought with him a hunger to recreate the memories and mood of Jamaican dance hall music. Those roots nourish rap.

David LaChapelle's film *Rise* highlights a specific kind of dancing that their inventors call "Krumping." It grows out of L.A. street culture. Tommy Johnson, known as "Tommy the Clown," developed a unique dance form, which he called "Clowning," in response to the 1992 L.A. riots, as an aesthetic form of highly skilled, athletically charged, speed-driven movement viewed as an alternative to gang warfare. One set of movements exchanged for the other, so to speak. "Clowning" morphed into "Krumping," and it definitely draws on African tribal rituals.

Black artists used Abstract Expressionism and social protest — and brushes, pens, invented materials, and found objects — to fashion the textures and colors of a new black humanity that challenged racial stereotypes. Our humanity shines in Elizabeth Catlett's *Sharecropper*, a portrait of a black woman that conjures strength and elicits sympathy. It is glimpsed as well in Bettye Saar's *The Liberation of Aunt Jemima*, a feisty revision of the black mammy myth, and in Kara Walker's black-cut paper silhouettes, including *Insurrection! (Our Tools Were Rudimentary, Yet We Pressed On)*, which play with racial stereotypes to undercut them.

The purpose of art is not simply to embrace and coddle, or to affirm and to edify. Artists are also supposed to be irreverent, and to poke fun at pieties, and to force people to think more critically about themselves.

Dave Chappelle looked like he was crazy because he made a sane decision: "I will not allow money to define my maturity or my mental health. I will walk away from fifty million dollars before I will sacrifice my integrity." And people thought he was crazy because he turned the money down. They didn't think he was sane because he made a choice that he would not be a servant of the very thing that alienated him from his craft. You don't have to be a Marxist economist to understand that if you're alienated from the work that you love and produce, then you're alienated from yourself. Chappelle simply wanted to reconnect to his art and the spiritual inspiration that motivated him to create in the first place. If a brother steps up and says, "Look, I ain't gonna be a slave to a contract, but I want to be my own man, my own comedian, my own artist, and I want to stand up and represent as best I can," he shouldn't be thought of as crazy.

Jewish comedy in the '30s, '40s, and '50s really set an incredibly high standard that continues to define how we understand what's funny in America today. What's remarkable, of course, is that an ethnic group that was being mistreated and oppressed in the larger society seized this medium of cultural expression and expanded the boundaries of Jewish identity even as they translated their experience into universal terms that were appreciated by the masses. Their success is summed up in that old Jewish saying in entertainment, especially in comedy, that goes something like "think Yiddish and write goyish." The insecurities, idiosyncrasies, and ingenuities of Jewish identity were brilliantly compressed into a brand of comedy that built on sharp social observation, self-deprecation, and relentless signifying. From Jack Benny to Milton Berle, from Shecky Green to Alan King, from Jerry Lewis to Jerry Seinfeld, from Lenny Bruce to Robert Klein, from Gracie Allen to Penny Marshall, from George Burns to Billy Crystal, and from the Borscht Belt to Broadway, Jewish comedians have injected profound moral, aesthetic, and spiritual qualities into American comedy, transforming it with their own views of human identity and existence.

———

There's no question that the most gifted figures in the Black Arts Movement (BAM), including Larry Neal, Hoyt Fuller, Amiri Baraka, Nikki Giovanni, and Sonia Sanchez, understood that politics was central to artistic vision. The Black Arts Movement, which lasted from the mid-'60s through the mid-'70s, argued that art is a servant of the masses. In BAM there was a great effort to make literature accessible to everyday black folk, especially through live poetry performances. BAM also brought art to the masses through the plays of figures like Ed Bullins, who penned *In the Wine Time,* and Amiri Baraka's *Dutchman.* Bullins's work led to the founding of the New Lafayette Theatre (NLT), and Baraka's play helped to establish the Black Arts Repertory Theatre/School (BART/S), the fruit of BAM's beliefs. And the visual art of the Black Arts Movement was intended to help clarify the esoteric meanings and abstract images of experimental Afro-expressionism, showing how they were rooted in black resistance and liberation — from Ademola Olugebefola's 1968 work *Space Dance* to Lev Mills's 1972 collage *I'm Funky, but Clean.*

———

I'm a huge Hannah Arendt fan. I went to see, in New York, the Kate Fodor play, *Hannah and Martin,* that dramatizes the relationship between Arendt and her mentor, and later her lover, Martin Heidegger. There are so many moments where her brilliance is blistering. In that Eichmann book she wrote, she talks about "the banality of evil," how evil has been made routine, even acceptable. And that has been an incredibly important concept for me in trying to explain how the *groundless grotesque*, and the *transcendent tragic*, can get reduced to routine, to the quotidian, to everyday stuff that comes out as pathology. So her work has been very important to me.

––––––––

Anna Deavere Smith's play *Fires in the Mirror* is a haunting portrait of the small agreements and large grievances between blacks and Jews. Smith's characters reveal the rituals and values that hold racial communities together in crisis (in this case, the death of a black boy struck by a car driven by Hasidic Jews in Brooklyn, and the subsequent Crown Heights riots during which a Hasidic scholar was killed by a black youth). Smith's poignant vignettes explore racial difference without lapsing into a simplistic vision of universality — of how we can all get along. Smith forces us to take stock of our conditions as people. She invites us to confront the racial, social, and cultural events that bind us, even if loosely, around a core of meaningful beliefs and behaviors. And she shows how we all hunger for stability in a rapidly changing world. Refusing to impose lessons from above, Smith allows the moral worldviews of fractured, and often opposed, communities to register in their own words — sometimes harsh and bitter, but always honest and uncompromising.

––––––––

The politics of race percolate in rock maverick Stew's stirring and introspective musical *Passing Strange*. The conceit of the play is the pursuit of The Black Real, or how black folk define what's racially and culturally authentic. That's a question that vexes both hardcore rappers and, quite obviously, prophets and politicians. In Stew's hands, it's at the heart of the various explorations of blackness of a young rock musician as he traipses from his native haunt of '70s Los Angeles, where he was filled with religious ideas of purity and danger, to Amsterdam's sense of free love, and on to '80s Berlin political agitprop. The play ingeniously weaves together high culture and pop culture to discuss authentic blackness and who can be said to own it. As the narrator says, he is concerned with the "reinvention, transformation and the limits of blackness." Or as one song's chorus contends, "I let my pain **** my joy and I call the bastard art." To put forth a black rock musician to help understand authentic blackness is complex and irreverent, and challenges cultural insiders and outsiders alike.

August Wilson brilliantly explored the terrain of twentieth-century black life in a series of plays whose sheer elegance is a testimony to the black will to survive the worst that life offers.

Alvin Ailey's dance troupe — especially in the sweep of Judith Jamison's limbs — won appreciation for the grace of black movement, even as the rhythms of black tap created a heartbeat through the soles of Sammy Davis, Jr., Gregory Hines, and Savion Glover.

Break dancing was the attempt to take preexisting forms and movement — especially Brazilian caopoeira — and fuse them with New York street style as a marker of identity. It was a way of saying, "I'm going to take the breaks of life and use them creatively." The breaks in the music were taken by the DJs in one direction — expanded and looped to form a new musical expression from an existing musical form — and in another direction by dancers, who used the musical experimentation with break beats to create dances that incorporate a variety of ethnic gestures. The break — something relatively minor in the musical arsenal — has now been highlighted and made a major creative element.

Not all of us can sing or dance well, but all of us can sing our own songs, dance our own dances, and support artists whose views reflect our values. Artists play a critical role by doing what they do, and if they do more than that — like being socially and politically active — then it's a blessing, bonus, and boon.

In an earlier era, the exotic Southern black supposedly had more soul, was closer to nature as a semi-literate savage, could sing and dance well, was more innately spiritual, was oblivious to the caste system that kept her in poverty, and hence, was happy to be the white Southerner's slave, servant, or entertainer. The art created by poor blacks was rarely recognized by whites unless it confirmed crude stereotypes of black sensual longing and intellectual emptiness. The complex and demanding creations of poor blacks, whether a sophisticated blues lyric or a visual art piece of high quality, was either dismissed or ignored, or at best, seen as exceptional to the inferior work of other black artists.

Two photos helped shape perceptions of race in the aftermath of Hurricane Katrina. In the first photo, a young black man clasps items in each arm as he forges through the flood waters. The caption to the AP (Associated Press) photo of him reads: "A young man walks through chest deep flood water after *looting a grocery store*" in New Orleans. In the second photo, also from AP, a·young white man and woman tote food items in their hands as they carry backpacks and slush through the flood waters, as the caption accompanying their photograph reads: "Two residents wade through chest-deep water after *finding bread and soda from a local grocery store*" after Hurricane Katrina landed.

The captions help lend value, and a slant, to essentially neutral photographs, pictures which, on their own, suggest solidarity of circumstance between the black and white youth. But the identical character of their experience is shattered by the language which casts their actions in contrasting lights: the white youth have been favored by serendipity and thus "naturally" exploit their luck in "finding" food, a gesture which relieves them of culpability; the black youth, by comparison, has interrupted the natural order of things to seize what didn't belong to him and thus remains responsible for his behavior. How black folk are "framed" — how we are discussed, pictured, imagined, conjured to fit a negative idea of blackness, or called on to fill a slot reserved for the outlaw, thug, or savage — shapes how we are frowned on or favored in mainstream society.

Back then, in 1984, in a failed Orwellian future, when we lived in a less sophisticated technological era where we couldn't get music through a quick download or file sharing over the Internet, we had to do it the old-fashioned way: stand before "The Stereo" and place the stylus over the rotating, compressed wax and allow the analog vibrations to brush across our soundscape and through our nearly busted woofers and tweeters. Crackles and snaps surged through the speakers, and the needle rapidly unraveled the tightly configured lines on the album's black face — and no matter how expertly you cleaned your vinyl disc it was bound to emit faint noises from a sharp object impressing a moving, flat surface.

The Motown Museum is chock-full of memorabilia drawn from an era when black entrepreneurial ingenuity met transcendent talent. Together, these forces transformed music into history in a city whose cultural and economic motors were not yet stalled by postindustrial collapse, gentrification, carjacking, white flight — and black track — to the suburbs, and political corruption. Those small rooms and humble instruments, which produced such big results, remind me of just how much of a David-versus-Goliath story Motown really was. And seeing Berry, Michael, Diana, Marvin, Smokey, and Claudette, the Temps, the Four Tops, and the rest of the crew in black-and-white photos recalls an era of faux innocence tragically shattered later in de-Africanized faces, infanticide, egomaniacal ambition, ripped-off royalties, and chemical slavery.

There's a way in which Jewish comedy, in terms of its vast ranges of signification, has now become American comedy. The genius of Jewish comedy is to be able to translate Yiddish idiosyncrasy — and an engagement with their particular marginal slice of the world — into what America is about. Sarah Silverman has been cut off in a certain way. We don't understand her signification. We don't understand the modes through which she expresses her sense of irreverence or irony or parody, because we're not used to women at a certain level doing that. When we discuss Sarah Silverman's art and craft, we can talk about Jewish comedians, about female comedians, and even about Jewish female comedians in particular. But the reality is that women don't get the chance to be that ironic or parodic in a way that signifies on stereotypes like Ali G can. I think it's partly gender. But also, her comedy moves in two directions because she's trying to force Jews to think critically about their own stereotyping, and about how they're being stereotyped. And that give-and-take, that kind of postmodern Jewish irreverence, may not go over well with some folk.

If the comic of color can't help being representative, it is because she embodies in her art the turmoil and suffering that anonymous blacks regularly endure without the platform or public sympathy the celebrity comic may enjoy. The black comic need not surrender a complex or independent vision of black identity to uphold her critical function; part of the appeal of black comics is their irreverent perspectives that encourage pitiless cultural inventory and relentless self-critique.

There are dialects and vernaculars within comedy, but in the end, humor is a universal language that can be understood by everyone. Black folk can watch and enjoy *Seinfeld* with its inside ethnic humor and its accessible jokes, and whites can watch *The Cosby Show* and appreciate both its racial accents and its universal themes.

Postmodernism may turn out to be modernism in drag.

In *Do the Right Thing,* Spike Lee's neonationalism leaps off the screen through brilliant cinematography and riveting messages. *Do the Right Thing* contains symbols of racism and resistance to racism, representations of black life, and images of black nationalist sensibilities and thought. Lee creates symbols that reveal the remorseless persistence of racism in quotidian quantity, exposing the psychopathology of everyday racism as it accumulates in small doses, over the course of days not unlike the one we witness in *Do the Right Thing.* Lee shows us the little bruises, the minor frustrations, and the minute but myriad racial fractures that mount without healing. Lee's decision to provoke discussion about racism is heroic. He exposes a crucial American failure of nerve, a stunning loss of conscience about race.

With John Singleton's *Boyz N the Hood* we have the most brilliantly executed and fully realized portrait of the coming-of-age odyssey that black boys must undertake in the suffocating conditions of urban decay and civic chaos. Singleton adds color and depth to Michael Schultz's groundbreaking *Cooley High,* extends the narrative scope of the Hudlin brothers' important and humorous *House Party,* and creates a stunning complement to Gordon Parks's pioneering *Learning Tree,* which traced the painful pilgrimage to maturity of a rural black male. Singleton's treatment of the various elements of contemporary black urban experience — gang violence, drug addiction, black male-female relationships, domestic joys and pains, friendships — is subtle and complex. He layers narrative textures over gritty and compelling visual slices of black

culture that show us what it means to come to maturity, or
die trying, as a black male.

———

Dennis Hopper perceptively, and provocatively, helped
probe the anomie and rebellion for a whole generation of outsiders in 1969's *Easy Rider,* though his film about gang warfare in Los Angeles, *Colors,* less successfully traces the
evolution of social despair, urban absurdity, and yearning for
belonging that shed light on gang violence.

———

In his magnum opus, *Malcolm X,* the greatest black biopic
ever made, Spike Lee has poignantly and insightfully rendered the life of an American original. Above all, in taking the
risk of defining and interpreting a controversial figure, he has
sent us back into our own memories, or to books and docu-
mentaries, in search of the truth for ourselves. And he has
done more than that. He has set the nation talking about a
figure whose life deserves to be discussed, whose achievements deserve critical scrutiny, and whose career merits the
widest possible exposure. Many great films have achieved
considerably less than that.

———

Matty Rich's *Straight Out of Brooklyn* is a desolate rejection
of liberal democracy: that individuals can act to realize themselves and enhance their freedom in the community or the
state. For the inhabitants of Brooklyn's Red Hook Housing
Project, self-realization and freedom are stunted by the menacing ubiquity of the ghetto. Rich's film rejects all pretensions
that the ghetto is not a totalizing force. It argues that it's impossible to maintain the boundaries between geography and

psychic health implied by the expression "Live in the ghetto, but don't let the ghetto live in you." It is precisely in showing that the ghetto survives parasitically — that its limits are as small or as large as the bodies it inhabits and destroys — that *Brooklyn* achieves for its auteur a distinct voice among black filmmakers.

———

Mario Van Peebles's ghetto in *New Jack City* is a sinister and languid dungeon of human filth and greed that is cartoonish and campy. The sheer artifice of *New Jack City*'s ghetto is meant to convey the inhuman consequences of living in a zone of civic horror, but its overdrawn dimensions suggest a closer resemblance to '70s blaxploitation flicks than to neorealist portrayals of ghetto carnage in other recent black ghetto films.

———

In *Juice,* director Ernest Dickerson's moral strategy is to explore the fatal logic of the gang as a family unit, a faulty premise that overlooks the destructive consequences when there are no moral constraints. Dickerson's artistic strategy is to move the cameras with the action from the observer's frame of reference, borrowing a few pages from Spike Lee's book (he has photographed many of Lee's films) without mimicking Lee's penchant for throwing the observer off with unusual angles and the fast pace of editing. Dickerson gently, then insistently, draws us into his moral worldview; it is an invitation to view the spectacle of black male loss of love by degrees and effects.

———

The Hughes brothers' brilliant, disturbing 1992 debut, *Menace II Society,* reveals the absurdity and terror that dog young black males. Their terse, lean script — complemented by the cast's surprising economy of emotional expression, given the genre's tendency to trumpet more than whisper — sharply contrasts with the harsh realities the film reveals: postindustrial urban collapse, the destructive personal and social effects of drug economies, and the violence of everyday black male life in urban America.

—————

In many ways, Mario Van Peebles's *Panther* (based on a screenplay penned by his legendary father, Melvin Van Peebles) captures black nostalgia for the days before crack and crime gutted black neighborhoods, before the quest for upward mobility trampled the fires of revolution. Although *Panther* creatively joins fiction to fact, anyone familiar with the period can see that the film is bold, revisionist history. The results are edifying and disturbing. The film accents some neglected truths while avoiding others, proving that cinematic imagination can be empowered or poorly served by a selective memory. The film unabashedly favors the Panthers' perspective: it focuses on how they got started, what their goals were, and how they pursued them. In so doing, *Panther* adds the name of Mario Van Peebles to those of Oliver Stone and Spike Lee, directors who deny that history can be seen objectively. For these directors, film is inherently political; it's about taking sides and making points. While some of their movies bravely correct the fictions in accepted accounts of events, they also wear blinders of their own.

—————

As *Bulworth*'s star, director, and co-writer, Warren Beatty uses gangsta rap's erotically charged violence and vulgar speech, both literally and metaphorically, to reveal the corruption of electoral politics. Beatty is not only flipping the script. He's unabashedly embracing an art form that has been scorned by white politicians and by the black bourgeoisie. In colorful and comedic terms, *Bulworth* shows how the social rituals and cultural conventions of gangstas and politicians are driven by the same goals: getting paid, getting pleasure, and getting props.

———

Realism in film is not made by taking a camera and training it on a block for a week and calling it a film. Realism depends on artifice and fiction to create its effect.

———

Hustle & Flow is to pimpdom what Clint Eastwood's *Unforgiven* is to the Western: a visual unmaking and cinematic undoing of the very mythology on which the pimp rests. *Hustle & Flow* demythologizes the pimp narrative and mythology, 'cause the pimp is poorer than his hoes! So the film twists the literal dependence of the pimp upon his hoes (after all, the pimp depends on the economic earning power of his stable of women) to a spiritual and moral dependence. It's like he's a pimp who's got his game on layaway, and his hoes are going to get him out of debt. Or it's like he's a pimp with his game in a pawn shop, and his hoes are going to get him out of hock. Furthermore, this is a po' broke pimp with a bootleg car, with a "hooptie." One of the most powerful and potent phallic symbols — in pimping and in other masculine domains — is the car. This pimp got a broke down ride! He ain't got no air

conditioning. I don't want to make this a feminist tale, because it still takes place within the context of a pimp-ho relationship. But that being said, it's remarkable to what degree
DJay, the film's pimp, relies on the intellectual insights of his
hoes — whether it's his baby's mama, Shug, who is providing
the hook for his raps, and a lava lamp for inspiration, or the
white ho, Nola, who always wanted to be more than a mere
ho, who eventually takes over DJay's rap business while he's
in jail.

———————

People throughout the world resonated with Tupac's powerful artistic vision, a vision, I believe, that joined him to
artists and intellectuals like Samuel Beckett, Zora Neale
Hurston, Eugene Ionesco, Simone de Beauvoir, Langston
Hughes, Hannah Arendt, Paul Robeson, Frantz Fanon, and
Simone Weil, since they, like Tupac, sought to find a legitimate voice through developing their gifts. People around the
globe felt Tupac's spirit, felt his love, his passion, his anger,
his rage, his confusion, and the chaos of the conflicting ideals
that engulfed him. Above all, Tupac identified with the underdog, and that gave him cachet among the world's downtrodden and those who faced huge odds, from poverty to political
oppression. Tupac represented and spoke to that brother, that
sister, that human being who in the face of enormous crisis
called on God, spirit, transcendent artistic and moral figures,
and their own passion as a resource to fight the destruction,
suffering, pain, and even death they encountered.

MED

chapter 10

Gender

We've got to grapple with instances of internalized sexism in women where the ventriloquist magic of patriarchy is occurring — women's lips are moving, but men's voices and beliefs are speaking.

Femiphobia — the fear and disdain of the female.

———

We've got to grapple with instances of internalized sexism in women where the ventriloquist magic of patriarchy is occurring — women's lips are moving, but men's voices and beliefs are speaking.

———

A great deal of the nation's gender problem has to do with how men think about women. Such thinking is largely rooted in the belief that God has set up a hierarchy where women fall beneath men in the natural order of things. But I think it's long past time that we reexamine our beliefs and come up with different ideas about how things work, and how we should behave in light of what we learn.

———

Black women have been a defining force in our liberation struggles, so we shouldn't seek to oppress the very sisters who valiantly helped to win our freedom as a people, and as *black men*.

———

We must battle those who use the Bible to justify some terrible beliefs about black women. We get awfully upset — and rightfully so — with how hip hop culture demeans and degrades sisters. We are outraged when a rapper resorts to epithets to disrespect our women, and despite my great love for hip hop, I'm sympathetic to that critique. But at the same time, we permit some destructive ideas to flourish in the church. These ideas are harmful because they influence how we act, not only in church, but also in our homes and schools.

We've got to find a new way to behave so that our children inherit a more positive future.

Black men can love black women by promoting the biblical principle of *mutual* submission contained in the fifth chapter of Ephesians. Mutual submission means that we act in a way to enhance the interests of each partner in the relationship. The text topples the notion that men should rule over a woman's life in home or society. Our liberating black religion teaches us that nobody has ultimate authority over our lives but God.

When most of our white brothers and sisters hear the word "race," they think "black" or "brown" or "yellow" or "Native American." They don't think "white," as if white is not one among many other racial and ethnic identities. Men are the same way. When black men hear male supremacy, we often think, "white guys who control the world." We don't think, "black guys who control our part of the world."

Black men have to surrender our patriarchal pose and our sexist strut. In our homes, that means that we've got to listen to and learn from our women as we strengthen our relationships. We must respect one another, encourage one another, sacrifice for one another, and stand up for one another, even against harmful gender ideas we've supported over the years.

A lot of black men are afraid to love black women with abandon because we fear they won't recognize the hurts that black men face. But nothing could be further from the truth. In fact, black women have been among the most vocal and progressive advocates for black men. Who was way out front on the issue of the prison-industrial complex that affects the million black men locked away, many unfairly, and to warn us about the injustice of incarceration? Angela Davis. Who edited the book that rigorously explored the claim that black males are an endangered species? Jewelle Taylor Gibbs. And who sang a song about the destructive images of black men in the culture and praised us for our moral beauty and our strength? Angie Stone.

———

We don't have to disrespect or dominate our women to feel like men.

———

Black men must be careful not to justify our ugly treatment of black women by pointing to our pain. We must avoid what the scholar Barbara Christian calls "the oppression derby," where groups argue over who has suffered the most. Black men can't pretend that our oppression is worse than black women's. Neither can we take solace in our suffering as a way to excuse our brutality toward our sisters. We cannot have a hierarchy of pain. If it hurts, it hurts. All of our pain is legitimate and real — if it is legitimate and real. So let's not waste any more time building a totem pole of catastrophe where we cut our niche of misery deeper or higher than black women's.

———

In a world where black women are battered by negative half-truths in the media, and ambushed by brutal put-downs from their own children in entertainment, the least we can do is to wrap sisters in the healing garments of reverence and respect.

———————

Black men must not be intimidated by the strength and intensity of our women's speech. Some women have had their voices muffled for so long that they shout when they can finally speak up. We should even encourage them to take "voice lessons" as they join with other women in amplifying their interests and desires.

———————

We can't lean on male supremacy to resolve conflicts or settle disputes in our homes. Instead, we've got to appeal to reason and to prayer, to negotiation and to consultation, to iron out our differences.

———————

A new understanding of black male and female relationships that can truly help our communities should flow from our churches. I believe that the black church is still the greatest institution black folk have, and we've got to work hard to keep it that way. That means we've got to move beyond the spiritual apartheid we practice. Seventy-five percent of the black church is made up of women, and yet they rarely have access to the central symbol of power — the pulpit. We've got to stop dragging our feet and begin to acknowledge just how important black women are to our churches — and to our mosques, temples, ashrams, and sanctuaries of all sorts. We must also realize just how important black women are to our success and survival as a people.

———————

We've got to sacrifice the unfair privileges we've gained by being men and seek to share power and responsibility with our partners. We've got to be willing to argue our case, but also to hear a case argued, as we make critical decisions that affect our relationships.

———

If I dislike myself, if I dishonor myself, if I hate myself, I will dislike, dishonor, and hate my partner. If I refuse to take care of myself, I threaten the quality of my relationship. If I hate myself I damage the person about whom my partner deeply cares. If I fail to appreciate the gifts God gave me I deny their expression to my partner, and perhaps, the world. If I have a low estimation of myself, I obviously believe my partner's judgment of me is distorted. That is a weak foundation on which to build any enduring relationship. That means that black male self-hate is hatred of black women. And black male hatred of black women is ultimately self-hatred. So the "bitch" we black men really hate may be staring back at us in the mirror.

———

Pimping mimics chattel slavery, or owning bodies to garner wealth. Pimping is the plantation in a Cadillac.

———

To compare the circumstances of poor black men and women is to compare our seats on a sinking ship. True, some of us are closer to the hub, temporarily protected from the fierce winds of social ruin. And some of us are directly exposed to the vicious waves of economic misery. But in the final analysis, we're all surviving or going down together.

———

We've got to reckon with forms of male privilege that thrive because we don't acknowledge them. Male privilege is strongest (so strong, in fact, that it was one of the first things that white men permitted black men to share with them) when we don't question it. We insulate ourselves from knowledge of its existence, especially when we take refuge in *our* oppression, as if that could prevent us from dealing with how we oppress more vulnerable folk.

I think black women have learned to absorb the pain of their predicament and to keep stepping. They've learned to take the kind of mess that black men won't take, or feel they can't take, perhaps never will take, and to turn it into something useful, something productive, something toughly beautiful after all.

Black feminist activity has been hampered by black women's loyalty to black men, often at the expense of their own interests and identities.

Some of the same arguments directed at Anita Hill in her charge of sexual harassment against Clarence Thomas are being used against the young women who protested rapper Nelly's visit to Spelman College's campus because of his sexist video "Tip Drill." Some critics claim that it took their generation too long to speak out, and that they were attacking a "good" black man like Nelly who was far from the worst sexist in hip hop. The same fault lines within the race that got revealed in the Thomas-Hill affair have traced beneath the Spelman-Nelly dispute. Another generation of black women acting in defense of themselves causes problems for patriarchal authority.

Historically, it has been difficult for black men to understand that although we're victims, we also victimize; that although we're assaulted, we also assault; and that while we're objects of scorn, we scorn black women as well. As with all groups of oppressed people, it's never a clean-cut matter of either/or; it's both/and. You can be victimized by white supremacy and patriarchy and at the same time extend black male supremacy.

Black men are also victims of male supremacy, patriarchy, sexism, and misogyny. Those horrible traits actually make *us* worse men. The profound investment in a violent masculinity costs many black men their lives, especially on the streets where codes of respect are brutally enforced. Closer to home, many black men turn violent on their loved ones, striking them instead of fighting a punishing social order for whom their wives, or girlfriends, or babymamas, or children are the unfortunate proxy.

Black men who can't get good jobs often blame their women who are employed.

Religious rhetoric was segregated by gender in the black church. There were unspoken yet inflexible rules that governed when and where women could speak. The pulpit and the deacon's bench were strictly off-limits. I had seen ministers fall into utter conniptions if a woman so much as glanced too strongly at the hallowed ground that was to be traversed only by "God's man." Thankfully, the Sunday School class, trustee board, vacation Bible school, Sunday pre-service testimonial, and prayer meeting were acceptable arenas of female speech.

Real men aren't afraid of real women.

A disturbing trend has gripped black America: young black males love their mamas but hate their "babymamas" in public. One of the reasons black males are violently vocal in conflicts with the mother of their children is that they're often young when fatherhood comes calling. Teen fathers who are barely grown themselves may lack the maturity to handle their beefs in private. As a former teen father with a turbulent first marriage, I know firsthand how arguments between young parents can slip easily into public view. Fortunately, I had a caring father and a pastor who counseled me not to resolve domestic differences on the sidewalk.

In patriarchy, women are often blamed for the limitations men impose on them. You hear this when young men justify the exploitation of women in rap videos: "Nobody is making these women appear in the videos; they must like it and want to do it." But that's like making early black actors the heavies when their only choice in movies was between stereotypical roles. It's not fair to blame those actors for the racist practices that limited their roles in the first place. Men should say, "*We* have limited the roles that black women can play in videos to dime piece, hoochie mama, video vixen, eye candy, arm pleasure, sexy dancer, and variations of the same." Instead, we blame women for accepting the crumbs from our sexist table. We force many of them to eat our patriarchal leftovers. That's a spiritually unbalanced meal.

———————

I'm hard pressed to tell the difference between Nelly's "Tip Drill" video and the time two hundred years ago when black women and men had their gluteus maximus, latissimus dorsi, pectoralis major, and their testicles examined so they could procreate and support slavery. Isolating body parts like that ties sexual fetish to the racist oppression of black bodies. It reinforces the vulgar status of black humanity, even when it has comic overtones like the troubling image created in the Nelly video.

———————

White culture venomously attacked black women long before the birth of hip hop. That helps to explain Don Imus's vulgar remarks that black members of the Rutgers University women's basketball team are "nappy-headed ho's." It is tragic that hip hop has done more than its share to spread such madness toward black females. Hip hop has made the assault on black women stylish. It has made sexism more acceptable by supplying linguistic updates, like the word "ho," to support deeply entrenched bigotry. Hip hop has helped desensitize our culture to the systematic attack on black women.

———————

The Spelman sisters who protested rapper Nelly's visit to their campus had to grapple with an unfair and absurd question put to activist black women through the ages: "Are you female first or are you black first?" The reality is that black women are black and female simultaneously — and in many cases, poor too. Identity isn't something one can parcel out. As feminist theorist Elizabeth Spellman memorably put it, we must not have an additive vision of identity, where you keep adding elements to increase your minority status — black, female, poor, lesbian, and so on. Still, you can't deny that black women have a lot of complex realities to confront in their bodies. Black women have displayed such extraordinary fidelity to the race that when they finally decide to speak up for themselves, they are viewed as traitors. Black men have often told black women that feminist concerns should only be addressed when the racial question is settled, but we all know that if black women wait that long, justice will never come.

MED

chapter 11

Preachers and Preaching

The preacher is the magnificent center of
rhetorical and ritualistic gravity in the black
church, fighting off disinterest with a "you
don't hear me," begging for verbal response
by looking to the ceiling and drolly declaring
"amen lights," twisting his body to reach for
"higher ground," stomping the floor, pounding
the pulpit, thumping the Bible, spinning
around, jumping pews, walking benches,
climbing ladders — yes literally — opening
doors, closing windows, discarding robes,
throwing bulletins, hoisting chairs, moaning,
groaning, sweating, humming, chiding,
pricking, and edifying, all to better "tell the
story of Jesus and his love."

C. L. Franklin was a "down-home" preacher, a lionized pulpiteer whose homilies spread over seventy-six recordings that
found wide circulation in black communities throughout the
nation. Ironically, I had to go all the way to the country — to
the Alabama farm of my grandparents on which my mother
was reared, and where she picked cotton — to hear for the
first time the oratorical wizardry of a Detroit icon. I listened
raptly and repeatedly to Franklin's rhetorical gifts churning
through my grandfather's archaic portable record player. He
possessed a powerful voice with a remarkably wide range.
Franklin could effortlessly ascend to his upper register to
squeal and squall. He was equally capable of descending to a
more moderate vocal hum and pitch, and then, at a moment's
notice, he could recompose in dramatic whisper. The velocity
of his speech was no less impressive, too. Franklin was the
greatest exemplar of "whooping," or the "chanted sermon,"
where ministers coarsen their articulation, deliberately and
skillfully stress their vocal cords, and transition from spoken
word to melodious speech. He was the shining emblem of folk
poetry shaped in the mouth of a minister whose mind was
spry and keen. Franklin's style rarely undercut his substance.

———

Martin Luther King made speech a handmaiden of social
revolution.

———

Gardner Taylor's unique blend of gifts may place him at the
forefront of the greatest cadre of preachers. His mastery of
the technical aspects of preaching is remarkable. He brilliantly uses metaphor and has an uncanny sense of rhythmic
timing put to dramatic but not crassly theatrical effect. He
condenses profound biblical truths into elegantly memorable

phrases. He makes keen use of parallels to layer and reinforce the purpose of his sermons. His stunning control of narrative flow seamlessly weaves his sermons together. His adroit mix and shift of cadences reflects the various dimensions of religious emotion. He superbly uses stories to illustrate profound intellectual truths and subtle repetition to unify sermons. And his control of his resonant voice allows him to pliantly whisper or prophetically thunder the truths of the gospel. What was once alleged of Southern Baptist preacher Carlyle Marney may be equally said of Taylor: he has a voice like God's — only deeper. Taylor's magnetism lies in his intimate and unequalled command of the language and literature of the English-speaking pulpit.

In the best black oratory, style is not juxtaposed to argument; in fact, style becomes a vehicle of substance.

Throughout its history, black preaching has been widely viewed as a form of public address brimming with passion but lacking intellectual substance. Like black religion in general, black preaching is often seen as the cathartic expression of pent-up emotion, a verbal outpouring that supposedly compensates for low self-esteem or oppressed racial status. Not only are such stereotypes developed in ignorance of the variety of black preaching styles, but they don't take into account the black churches that boast a long history of educated clergy.

Jesse Jackson's words winced and winked in the battle against white supremacy, even as he returned fire with every weapon in his impressive rhetorical arsenal: gutbucket metaphors, urban parables, extended analogies, street slang, country grammar, theological sophistication, Southern diction, preacherly pacing, biting wit and humor, and an imperishable will to clarity. Jackson made love in language; he relished promiscuous verbal trysts with audiences around the world, flexing and undulating and twisting his meanings in an erotically agitated cadence that conjured the spirit and the flesh in the same breath. His rhyming speech was an unavoidable homage to Muhammad Ali and a forerunner to hip hop, as Jackson played rebel badass and strutting reverend with equal vigor. Jackson's verbal vitae also tentatively resolved in style what couldn't be bridged in philosophy or in person: Malcolm X's slashing and combative rhetorical fusillade and the high elegance of King's most finely wrought phrasing. Jackson also combined King's analytical sharpness with Ralph Abernathy's colorful down-home vernacular to offer engaging snapshots of the black condition.

James Weldon Johnson's classic poem "God's Trombones" provides a literary glimpse of the art and imagination of the black folk preacher. C. L. Franklin's recorded sermons, spread out over sixty albums for Chess Records, brought the vigor and ecstasy of the black chanted sermon — dubbed in black church circles as "the whoop" — to the American public. By and large, however, Americans have remained insulated from the greatest rhetorical artists of the black pulpit.

James Forbes deftly blends prophetic criticism and priestly patience. He possesses a sociospiritual acumen that addresses issues like racism, sexism, classism, and homophobia, while generating authentic pastoral responses to the people who both combat and embody these ills. As a professor of preaching at Union Theological Seminary, Forbes displayed a delightful zest for what many considered a dying art form. Under the discipline of a sanctified imagination, Forbes transformed the tedium of homiletics into an exciting adventure into the labyrinth of sacred speech. As a lecturer (most notably, in Yale's Beecher Lectures), conference speaker, and revival preacher, Forbes has crisscrossed America in pursuit of his vocation of making the word come alive. Forbes's high visibility as the first African American to fill the famed pulpit of New York's Riverside Church gave a hearing to the homiletical styles, rhetorical practices, and oral nuances of the best black preaching.

The competing public images of Al Sharpton — glorified racial ambulance chaser, racial poseur bent on stirring controversy, camera-hogging activist more interested in the limelight than civil rights — often ignore his Pentecostal roots and the influence on his style and approach by a diverse cadre of mentors. Sharpton, born in 1954, was a bona fide prodigy of the black pulpit: at the age of four, he began to extol the Lord's word in his Brooklyn Pentecostal church, and by the age of ten, the pint-sized preacher who had been dubbed the "Wonderboy" was officially ordained. Sharpton's bread and butter is turning the sacred spoken word to political use, using a sharp wit to underscore social suffering, dramatizing social injustice through bold public gestures, and projecting black leadership through an ethic of swagger. Sharpton is a man of enormous gifts, a former wunderkind of black homiletics who fulfilled his early promise with a biting, brilliant tongue in defense of the vulnerable, and with a skilled and inventive leadership that, at its best, extends the legacy of King and Jackson.

The prosperity gospel movement is obsessed with getting rich and reading the Bible through an exclusively entrepreneurial lens. The prophetic refrain of the black pulpit, as marginal as it has always been, is even more silenced in entrepreneurial evangelism. Prosperity gospel's most zealous proponents say that God wants all believers to drive big cars and live in big houses and make big money. Instead of criticizing excess, they rabidly embrace it; they slight altogether the structural forces that sustain poverty. Entrepreneurial evangelists personalize poverty; the poor either rise to riches or fall to being broke by their own sweat and prayers. It's self-help dispensed from a Mercedes-Benz or a private jet.

Broad segments of American society have sampled the richness of black preaching through the brilliant political oratory of Martin Luther King, Jr., and Jesse Jackson. Both King's and Jackson's styles of public speech — their impassioned phrasing, intellectual acuity, and imaginative metaphors — reflect their roots in the black church. And their involvement in civil rights and politics extends the venerable tradition of black preachers serving as social critics and activists. But their oratory — like that of preacher-politicians from Adam Clayton Powell to William Gray — has been shaped by the peculiar demands of public life and informed by a mission to translate the aspirations of black Americans to the larger secular society. The aims of their public speech have led them to emphasize certain elements of the black preaching and church traditions such as social justice, the institutional nature of sin, and the redistribution of wealth, while leaving aside such others as the cultivation of the spiritual life, the nurturing of church growth, and the development of pastoral theology. Such varying emphases are usually framed as the difference between "prophetic" and "priestly" religion. If the former has been most visible to American society in the guise of church-based civil rights activists, the latter has been closer to the heart of the religious experience of most black Christians.

For all of its problems and limitations, the black pulpit, at its best, is still the freest, most powerful, most radically autonomous place on earth for black people to encourage each other in the job of critical self-reflection and the collective struggle for liberation.

Black preachers collect sermons with the zeal of avid fans of baseball cards. At conventions of black denominations, the CDs of famous ministers sell briskly. These CDs are especially circulated and reproduced among younger preachers, serving as models of preaching excellence and training in the high art of sacred speech. Some even preach the sermons to their own congregations, trying out fresh ideas and new words they have gleaned from master storytellers. Frederick Sampson's "Dwelling on the Outskirts of Devastation," Jeremiah Wright's "Prophets or Puppets," Gardner Taylor's "A Wide Vision Through a Narrow Window," Charles Adams's "Sermons in Flesh," William Jones's "The Low Way Up," and Caesar Clark's "Elijah Is Us" have all acquired canonical status in a genre of religious address that treats the plight of the preacher.

Paying attention to how you say what you say doesn't mean you have nothing to say.

Frederick G. Sampson was an American original, a tall, commanding, impossibly literate dark-brown prince of the pulpit who lived up to that title when it still resonated in the world of homiletics. Sampson believed that those who breathed the life of the mind must serve the people in whose womb they came to exist. His thinking made sense to me because of how faithfully he adhered to his own principle. He wasn't a preacher who festooned his pulpit oratory with violent grunts or theatrical posing, though he was a verbal master with dramatic flair. Sampson unabashedly laced his rhetoric with the theology and poetry and philosophy he ardently consumed. In the pulpit, he moved effortlessly from Bertrand Russell to W. E. B. Du Bois, from Shakespeare to Paul Laurence Dunbar, and from the King's English spoken to the Queen's taste, to the wily black vernaculars that bathed the tongues of his Southern kinsmen. Outside the pulpit, Sampson's insatiable curiosity lead him to devour books and to traffic in ideas, wherever he could get good ones, whether from the mouth of a learned colleague or the neighborhood drunk. Critical encounter was nearly erotic to him, but the joy and passion he brought to intellectual life didn't obscure its necessary everydayness, its practical application, its edifying repetitiveness, and most of all, its usefulness to common folk.

Baptist preachers are always ripping each other off and using the stories, illustrations, phrases, verbal tics, mannerisms — and in some cases, whole sermons — we glean from other preachers. That's how we learn to preach; by preaching like somebody else until we learn to preach like ourselves, when our own voice emerges from the colloquy of voices we

convene in our homiletical imagination. And in the end, the
only justification for such edifying thievery among preachers
is that the Word is being preached and the ultimate author of
what we say is being glorified.

————————

Martin Luther King spoke much the way a jazz musician
plays, improvising from minimally or maximally sketched
chords or fingering changes that derive from hours of practice
and performance. The same song is never the same song, and
for King, the same speech was certainly never the same
speech. He constantly added and subtracted, attaching a
phrase here and paring a paragraph there to suit the situation.
He could bend ideas and slide memorized passages through
his trumpet of a voice with remarkable sensitivity to his audience's makeup. King endlessly reworked themes, reshaped
stories, and repackaged ideas to uplift his audience or drive
them even further into a state of being — whether it was compassion or anger, rage or reconciliation — to reach for justice
and liberation. King had a batch of rhetorical ballads, long,
blue, slow-building meditations on the state of race, and an
arsenal of simmering mid-tempo reflections on the high cost
of failing to fix what fundamentally ails us — violence, hatred,
and narrow worship of tribe and custom. King knew how to
play as part of a rhetorical ensemble that reached back in time
to include Lincoln and Jefferson and stretched across waters
to embrace Gandhi and Du Bois in Ghana. But he played
piercing solos as well, imaginatively riffing off themes eloquently voiced by black preachers Prathia Hall and Archibald
Carey. In the end, King brilliantly managed a repertoire of
rhetorical resources that permitted him to play an unforget-
table, haunting melody of radical social change.

————————

As a species of black scared rhetoric, *whooping* is characterized by the repetition of rhythmic patterns of speech whose
effect is achieved by variation of pitch, speed, and rhythm.
The "whooped" sermon climaxes in an artful abbreviation or
artificial stretching of syllables, a dramatic shift in meter, and
often a coarsening of timbre, producing tuneful speech. In
black worship, whooping is central to the performance of
black sacred rhetoric.

Black preachers coin phrases, stack sentences, accumulate
wise sayings, and borrow speech to convince black folk, as
the gospel song says, to "run on to see what the end is gonna
be."

Charles Adams was dubbed the "Harvard Whooper" because of an intellectual brilliance honed at Harvard Divinity
School that is joined to a charismatic folk preaching style
gained as a youth when he was immersed in the colorful cadences of black religious rhetoric. Adams's riveting sermonic
style is characterized by a rapid-fire delivery, keen analyses of
biblical texts, the merger of spiritual and political themes, a
far-ranging exploration of the varied sources of African American identity, and a rhythmic, melodic tone that rides above a
piercing rhetorical ensemble composed of deliberately stri-
ated diction, staccato sentences, variously stressed syllables,
alliterative cultural allusion, and percussive phrasing. Further,
Adams highlights the inherent drama of black religious rhetoric by embodying its edifying theatrical dimensions. As
preacher, he is both *shaman* and *showman*. In his brilliant
pulpit oratory, Adams nurtures the sacrament of performance: ordinary time and events are flooded with a theolog-

ical sense of drama and spectacle. Adams, for instance, not only preached a biblical story of a woman searching for a lost coin; he took a broom into the pulpit and dramatized the search for lost meaning in life and the need to reorder existential priorities. Adams is one of the foremost examples of black preaching's tremendous power, and of the baptism of language and imagination for religious ends.

Martin Luther King's speech was a clinic in the use of the vocal instrument to vibrate in swooping glissandos and poignant crescendos. King showed that there didn't have to be strife between *lexis* (style, such as metaphor) and *pisteis* (argumentation and proof) as there is in Aristotle's view of rhetoric.

The preacher often said things that most black folk believed but were afraid to say. He used his eloquence and erudition to defend the vulnerable and assail the powerful.

In a 1993 poll conducted by *Ebony* magazine naming the nation's fifteen greatest black preachers, Jeremiah Wright was second only to legendary pulpiteer the Rev. Gardner Taylor. Wright's preaching genius derives from a mix of numerous strengths. He is clearly one of the most intellectually sophisticated and scholarly ministers in the land, reading widely and thinking deeply about the pressing religious and social issues that occupy his literate sermons. He possesses a musical voice whose intonations are brilliantly regulated during the course of his sermon delivery, rising and falling as emotion and circumstance dictate. His diction is flawless, his articulation precise, and his universe of linguistic reference is international given his command of several languages. Neither is Wright afraid to resourcefully dip into the lexicon of his native black birth and shape the grammatical constructions of his people into the ethical eloquence for which our best prophets are justly celebrated. Wright moves effortlessly from the streets to the sanctuary in illustrating the social sweep of the Christian gospel. And he is unparalleled in the pulpit in framing theological reflection with the insights and nuances of black culture, the perfect embodiment of his church's motto: Unashamedly Black and Unapologetically Christian.

There is a humorous three-step rhetorical rule of citation by which many black Baptist preachers operate. The first time they repeat something they hear, they say, "Like *Martin Luther King* said . . ." The second time they repeat it, they say, 'Like *somebody* said . . ." The third time they repeat it, they say, "Like *I* always say . . ."

I try not to avoid difficult subjects as I preach, and sometimes what I say goes over like a brick cloud! Still, I try to seduce people into seeing things differently, as I make arguments about why the opposition to gay and lesbian folk, for instance, reeks of the same biblical literalism that smashed the hopes of black slaves when white slave masters deployed it. But I try to win the folk over first, by preaching "in the tradition," so to speak, warming them up first before I lower the boom. When I was a young preacher and pastor, one of my members told me, "You draw more flies by honey than vinegar." So I give honey before I give vinegar. I invite the folk to the progressive theological, ideological, and spiritual terrain I want them to occupy, but I try to issue that invitation in ways that won't immediately alienate them. And once they're there, they're a captive audience.

———

The preacher is the magnificent center of rhetorical and ritualistic gravity in the black church, fighting off disinterest with a "you don't hear me," begging for verbal response by looking to the ceiling and drolly declaring "amen lights," twisting his body to reach for "higher ground," stomping the floor, pounding the pulpit, thumping the Bible, spinning around, jumping pews, walking benches, climbing ladders — yes literally — opening doors, closing windows, discarding robes, throwing bulletins, hoisting chairs, moaning, groaning, sweating, humming, chiding, pricking, and edifying, all to better "tell the story of Jesus and his love."

———

Too often, parish ministers are caught in the grind of crucial "housekeeping" chores — marriages, funerals, administrative tasks, prayer meetings, and church business — and find, or take, little time to study the faith. While we love God with our hearts and souls, we often forget to love God with our minds. Mack King Carter is exemplary in his devout attention to critical inquiry. His sermons are models of theological gravitas. His sacred rhetoric fairly teems with a profound wrestling with the weighty, and contradictory, matters of faith and reason. Carter has never been afraid to stretch his congregation's spiritual imagination and to lift its theological I.Q. through demanding preaching and teaching.

———

Black preachers inspired their people to survive by skillful use of rhetoric. The way black preachers spoke about God convinced black folk that God's rule was unbroken by history's tragedies, and that black social and moral striving was a reflection of the divine will. The performance of religious rhetoric in a racial vein wasn't just for "form or fashion," as elders in the black church say. Black sacred speech wasn't simply about wedding style to substance; but style itself was an index of the peculiar experience of black people in the modern world as they worshipped God in hostile circumstances.

Prathia Hall's powerful preaching introduced me to the genius of black female homiletical artistry. She interwove biblical narratives with stories from her pioneering career as a civil rights activist. Hall often topped off her sermons with rhetorical flourishes and stylistic gestures gleaned from her Baptist brethren and refined in her feminist crucible. Her sermons also displayed a thrilling measure of the melodious speech of "the whoop" or the "chanted sermon." As ministers say in black church circles, she had "the learnin' and the burnin'."

MED

chapter 12

Race and Identity

We must not reduce the problems of race
to face and skin; we must also see them
in structure and system.

Race is not a card. It is a condition.

––––––––

Our goal should not be to transcend race, but to transcend the biased meanings associated with race. Ironically, the very attempt to transcend race by denying its presence reinforces the power to influence perceptions because it gains strength in secrecy. Like a poisonous mushroom, the tangled assumptions of race grow best in darkness. For race to have a less detrimental effect, it must be brought into the light and openly engaged as a feature of the events and discussions it influences.

––––––––

The paradox of our situation is that Americans are fatigued and fascinated by race.

––––––––

Proud of their roots, some blacks worship them. But roots should nourish, not strangle, black identity.

––––––––

Color can't be the basis for analyzing culture because some of the best insight on black folk has come from white brothers and sisters. Conversely, some of the most leaden and unimaginative interpretations of black life have come from black folk.

––––––––

Blackness has never really been about genetics anyway. That's because most black folk could point to somebody in their family tree who couldn't pass muster as pure Nubian ancestry. The varied skin shades testified to broad patterns of racial mixing that black folk took for granted. And trying to

reduce race — any race, but especially blackness — to a genetic calculation is nearly beside the point. What disturbs or
assures us about race has very little to do with blood or biology. Sure, your color can get you pulled over for driving your
Ferrari in a white neighborhood, and it can get you followed
in a store where they think you don't have enough plastic to
ring the cash register. But race plays out in the streets and in
our culture in a far more complicated way. It's about how you
use language, understand your heritage, interpret your history,
identify with your kin, and figure out your meaning and worth
to a society that places values on you beyond your control.

We must not reduce the problems of race to face and skin;
we must also see them in structure and system.

You might protest to a passing cab that you are a mixture
of many races, but he might keep going because you look like
you're black. But the cue he gets from your color isn't about
your pigment alone; it's about what that color means to him,
how it's been jammed into his mind with a slew of stereotypes
about what a person who looks like you is likely to do, namely
rob, cheat, or kill him. He didn't get that from a DNA swab;
he got that from talking heads on television seeking to warn
him about the carnage you might inflict — or, perhaps, from
the latest 50 Cent video.

We don't have to embrace our American identity at the expense of our race. The two are not mutually exclusive. We
simply have to overcome the limitations imposed upon race,

to make sure that neither privilege nor punishment are viciously, arbitrarily assigned to racial difference.

It is also true that white allies to racial emancipation have often sacrificed blood and body in refusing to be loyal to the oppressive meanings of whiteness.

There are at least three different strategies of black identity which are constantly in play to manage our lives on a cosmic level. These strategies offer the world a picture of how we understand our blackness. The first strategy is *accidental blackness;* we, by the accident of birth, simply happen to be black. In this strategy, our blackness is only the most obvious, not the most important, element of our identity. The second strategy of blackness is *incidental blackness;* we are proud to be black, but it is but one strand of our identity. Our blackness is surely important and valued, but it is not the only feature of our identity that occupies our minds. Finally, there is *intentional blackness;* we are proud of our blackness and see it as a vital, though not the exclusive, aspect of our identity. Our blackness is understood in its political forms and its social manifestations. These strategies permit black folk to operate in the world with a bit of sanity and grace. Black folk pass in and out of these strategies over a lifetime. And one can be intentionally black in one setting — say in a protest march against police brutality — and incidentally black at the company picnic. Circumstances and politics make all the difference in how and when these strategies of blackness play out.

Premarital sex and illegitimacy were staples of the white slave-owning sexual economy: slave masters pillaged and plundered young girls and women at will, and produced a constant stream of babies that would make the stereotypical pimped-out, family-fleeing, children-abandoning, absentee-fathering black male blush in embarrassment at his relatively low productivity.

When O. J. Simpson took that long, slow ride down the L.A. freeway in A. C. Cowlings's Bronco, it wasn't the first time he used a white vehicle to escape a black reality.

There has been a profound resegregation of American schools. More than seventy percent of black students in the nation attend schools that are composed largely of minority students. The segregation of black students is more than twenty-five points below 1969 levels, but there are still plenty of financially strapped schools that make a mockery of the judicial mandate for integrated education. White students typically attend schools where less than twenty percent of the student body comes from races other than their own. By comparison, black and brown students go to schools composed of fifty-three to fifty-five percent of their own race. In some cases, the numbers are substantially higher; more than a third of black and Latino students attend schools with a ninety- to one-hundred-percent minority population. In tandem with residential segregation, school resegregation amounts to little more than educational apartheid.

It has become fashionable among many critics to claim that the biggest harm to black America is self-imposed. Racism, it is claimed, has largely run its course, and now only the ambition and fortitude of black folk can save them; only their foolish reliance on old racial scripts can lead them astray. Blacks must bootstrap their way to prosperity like any other immigrant group that overcame obstacles to find its footing in the culture. What is lacking in this argument is that most blacks were not immigrants, they were slaves, and even after the core of the culture achieved freedom, they were set the kinds of obstacles — death, dismemberment, and denial of self — that no other immigrant group ever faced on these shores.

One of the problems with neoliberalism is that it writes the check of its loyalty to the black and Latino poor against the funds of conservative rhetoric and social policy.

Although one may not have racial intent, one's actions may nonetheless have racial consequence. One may agree with Barack Obama that there was no racial intent, no "active malice," in the response to Katrina, and hold the view that there were nonetheless racial consequences that flowed from the "passive indifference" of the government to "the least of these." Active malice and passive indifference are but flip sides of the same racial coin, different modes of racial menace that flare according to the contexts and purposes at hand. In a sense, if one conceives of racism as a cell phone, then active malice is the ringtone at its highest volume, while passive indifference is the ringtone on vibrate. In either case, whether loudly or silently, the consequence is the same: a call is transmitted, a racial meaning is communicated.

White offenders routinely get treated to a brand of justice that differs greatly from that meted out to blacks and other minorities. We need standards of justice, and punishment for offense, that are, like Fox News is supposed to be, fair and balanced. A criminal justice system is criminal when it is ruined by racial preference and white privilege.

You can be oppressed and still be doggin' somebody else who's lower on the totem pole.

The tragic reign of slavery for 250 years, the colossal efforts of the government and the legal system to extend white supremacy through Jim Crow law, and the monumental effort of black folk to resist these forces while redefining black identity have formed the rhythms, relations, and rules of race. The rhythms of race have largely to do with customs and cultural practices that feed on differences between racial groups. The relations of race have mostly to do with the conditions that foster or frustrate interactions between racial groups. The rules of race have to do with norms and behavior that reflect or resist formal barriers to social equality. The rhythms, relations, and rules of race have both defined the forces against which progress must be made and provided a measure of the progress achieved. They help us understand that even when fundamental changes in law and practice occur — say, the Fourteenth Amendment, the *Brown v. Board of Education* Supreme Court decision, or the Civil Rights Act of 1964 —

there is the matter of racial vision and imagination to consider. They help us see that racial terror has bled through the boundaries of law as surely as harmful racial customs and beliefs persist in deep pockets of a formally changed society.

The oversight of Latino, Native American, Vietnamese, and Filipino suffering in the catastrophe of Katrina not only reinforces, for the latter three groups, their relative invisibility in American culture, and for Latinos, their relative marginalization in the region. It shows as well that our analysis of minorities must constantly be revised to accommodate a broader view of how race and ethnicity function in the culture. As important as it is, the black-white racial paradigm simply does not exhaust the complex realities and complicated interactions among various minority groups and the broader society.

At their best, black leaders and thinkers have advocated self-help philosophy while condemning the tragic social conditions that make it necessary.

Most of the folk in this country are immigrants; it's just a matter of when you came. Scholars of immigration say that this is the fourth great wave of immigration. The first wave was the Western Europeans who founded the nation. The second wave was in the middle of the nineteenth century, when you had an Eastern European influx. Most Jews and Poles and Italians arrived in the mid-1800s, late 1800s, or early 1900s. And of course, the nation was undergoing profound industrialization then. The third stage included the first two decades of the twentieth century. When you think of Ellis Island — a million immigrants a year came to this country, largely from Europe. And the fourth wave since the 1980s — 20 million people, mostly from Asia and Central America, are coming to the nation. So there's an extraordinary expansion of what it means to be an American. *E Pluribus Unum* — "Out of Many, One."

———

Although most groups don't have to pay the heavy identity tax that blacks do for negative information circulating in the culture, it is still a gesture of racial maturity to embrace our complexity and tell the truth about the good and bad of black life.

———

Katrina's fury may have been race neutral, but not its effect: eighty percent of New Orleans' minority households lived in the flooded area, while the same was true for only fifty-four percent of the city's white population. The average household income of those in the flooded area trailed those who lived on New Orleans' higher ground by $17,000. Concentrated poverty rendered poor blacks much more vulnerable to the effects of natural disaster.

———

Too many black youth are being warehoused in substandard schools in poor communities until they are sent to prison in unjustly disproportionate numbers.

———

It is no small irony that identity politics were denounced as soon as race was debunked as a social myth. And once racial stereotypes were toppled, it made sense to challenge romantic views of minority identity. It is unsurprising that identity politics, political correctness, and multiculturalism came under attack just as minorities gained greater say-so in the culture. It is a good thing to forcefully criticize insular or fascist identity politics. But it is intellectually irresponsible to renounce all forms of group solidarity. It is politically self-serving to damn black pride while slighting the histories and struggles that make it necessary.

———

Racial stereotypes may contain strands of truth wrapped around knots of willful ignorance and deadly distortion.

———

Although Southern blacks and whites in many ways lived in wildly different worlds, they had too much in common to make their quarrel easy or clean. They were joined by the Bible and the ham hock, by culture and cuisine. In fact, a mirror version of the Southern way of life operated in black life, even if it reflected a struggle against the inferiority imposed on it by white society. Black self-hatred often stemmed from the fear that what whites believed about blacks might be true. Black guilt, on the other hand, had to do with the failure to demand dignity and respect. The self-loathing that resulted was a faithful barometer of the great need for black liberation. But many blacks, convinced they were inferior and undeserving of equality, shrank further into a cocoon of self-hatred, denying their fitness to participate in the fight for freedom since they would be unworthy of its good results. They reinforced their chronic loss of self-worth by avoiding the struggle to achieve it.

———

Like a camel on the loose, race has the capacity to do greater injury when we attempt to coop it up as opposed to when we let it run free.

———

Simple views of black life chase nuance and contradiction to the sidelines.

———

Identity politics has been going on from the get-go in American culture, indeed, in cultures the world over. Aristotle and Plato and their followers were ensconced in identity politics; Descartes and Kant and their followers were negotiating identity politics; Foucault and Derrida and their followers are embroiled in identity politics; and Julia Kristeva and Luce Irigaray and their followers are unquestionably involved in identity politics, though they, as I suspect the others I've named, would vehemently deny it. That's because many of them are, or were, caught in the dream of transcendental truth, Enlightenment reason, deconstructive practice, or semiotic analysis that, for the most part, severs questions of identity from questions of racial politics.

———

It is supremely ironic that, under the banner of universalism and "self-evident" rights, black folk fought to gain benefits of citizenship that turned out to be neither self-evident nor universal.

———

Immigration policies are directed against Jose. They are *not* directed against Jurgen. Because we want Jurgen to come over here and help us on the super-information highway, whereas we fear Jose wants to take our jobs!

***

One need not believe that racism completely denies black folk the freedom to act, to acknowledge that real victims do exist. It is true that black addiction to victimization has sometimes turned issues better suited to small claims court into federal cases. The exaggeration of perceived racial injury among some blacks has helped to ruin the sense of proportion that should make the identification of real suffering a fairly simple calculation. In truth, however, America has rarely *willingly* acknowledged, much less responded to, black grievances.

***

This is a painful paradox of race: that blacks must often be *rejected into* the American creed, that they are often included only after their alienation from America reveals America's alienation from its social ideals.

***

When you think of the *Father Knows Best* era — in the time of black-and-white TV that we now romanticize — Lassie had a television program, and Nat King Cole, a black man of enormous talent, on whose back Capitol Records was built, had a program that, due to racism, was cancelled and couldn't stay on television for a year!

***

A stereotype is a lazy assessment of the other, a sloppy projection of bias onto a vulnerable target.

***

What right did the North have to tell the South about racism when it couldn't acknowledge its own racial problems? At least the South came clean about its dirt. It consciously, if imperfectly, sought a way to live with the mess. The North, on the other hand, claimed that it was already clean, and thus largely sidestepped the always difficult task of fixing what doesn't appear to be broken.

In regard to race, we are living, as it's been said, in the United States of Amnesia. We've got to revoke our citizenship in what Joseph Lowery terms "the 51st state, the state of denial."

There's no way to deal with race without going through race; there's no way of overcoming race without taking race into account.

Hopefully, in a future that still appears too far away, whites who speak against unjust privilege and power will join oppressed people around the globe as we create a world where we can lay down the burden of race.

One of the great paradoxes of race is that whiteness is not exclusively owned or produced by whites. White is also black. As we discover how black whiteness is, we discover how interesting and intricate whiteness is. We discover how whites and blacks have cooperated in very shrewd ways to produce an alternate to oppressive whiteness.

We've got to avoid the trap of spiritual puniness and racial infantilism — and sidestep the pitfalls of a narrow black identity.

***

Blacks and Latinos should join hands when possible — around issues of unemployment and xenophobia, language and social stigmatization, and class and cultural prejudice. Neither group has the luxury of arguing over which is really more reasonable, needier, or more American.

***

Progressives have temporarily lost the battle of language; it is now the political and cultural right that has co-opted progressive metaphors of racism — as disease, as loss of vision, of conscience corrupted and turned against its highest ends — and won the right to tell the story of American race. Contemporary neoconservatives are drawn like vultures to pick over the terms they helped to defeat, like "racial fairness" and "equal playing ground," giving them the opposite meaning intended by their liberal creators.

***

Some black folk believe that because they're black, they will automatically know black history, life, and culture. But that belief is simply not true. One cannot by means of osmosis absorb from black environments the collective memory of the race, since it is not passed on through the membranes, or though the nucleus or mitochondria of cells of racial experience. One must learn about black culture and history through serious study.

***

When black folk stop obsessing about what our white brothers and sisters think — and start concentrating on what is just and righteous — we will not only love ourselves better, but we may discover that we've got far more allies among other races than we ever imagined.

———

The South was embroiled in the *ugly evident.* The ugly evident, or the obvious racism of the South, marched against the inconspicuous evil of the North.

———

O.J. — the figure, the trial, the spectacle, the aftermath — was a racequake. It crumbled racial platitudes. It revealed the fault lines of bias, bigotry, and blindness that trace beneath our social geography.

———

For many folk, excellence made blacks exceptions to, not examples of, their race. Ironically, to be thought of as an exception to the race still denied a pure consideration of individual merit. As long as race colored the yardstick, a real measurement of individual achievement was impossible. It is a bitter paradox that the evaluation of individual achievement that blacks yearned for was subordinated to a consideration of any achievement's impact on, and relation to, the race. Blacks were routinely denied the recognition of individual talent that is supposed to define the American creed. This history is barely mentioned now that blacks are made by critics to look as if they duck individual assessment while embracing group privilege.

———

The ideal of a color-blind society is a pale imitation of a greater, grander ideal: of living in a society where our color won't be denigrated, where our skin will be neither a badge for undue privilege nor a sign of social stigma. But we can strive for a society where each receives his or her just due, where the past in all its glory and grief is part of the equation of racial justice and social equality. Then we won't need to be blind to color, which in any case is a most morbid state of existence. Then we can embrace our history and ideals with the sort of humane balance that makes democracy more than a distant dream.

A two-tiered universe of perception rotates around an axis defined by race. While good fortune lights one side, despair darkens the other. It is rarely sunny at the same time in white and black America.

It is easy to understand how some blacks wanted to escape the demands of being representatives of The Race, its shining symbols. Standing in for the group was a burden. It was also risky. You could never be sure that your efforts were taken seriously. In fact, a law of inversion seemed to apply. For most blacks, only the negative acts seemed to count. Even the positive became a negative good: it only counted as a credit against black liability, against all the wrong things black folk inevitably did. The good you did simply meant that you, and by extension, all blacks, didn't mess up this time. When the good was allowed to count, it only underscored one's uniqueness, that one was not like other black folk.

When dealing with their peers, blacks are seen as fair —
that is, neutral, just, and transcending race — only when they
oppose perceived black interests.

It is stunning how much ignorance about what really happened in our racial past poisons present debates about race.
Of course, we don't benefit from a Joe Friday "just the facts,
ma'am" perspective of the past. There will be disputes about
the facts and what they mean. But we certainly need to work
as hard as possible to figure out what happened as we interpret the history of race.

Race and racism are not static forces. They mutate, grow,
transform, and are redefined in complex ways. We must grasp
the hidden premises, buried perceptions, and cloaked meanings of race as they show up throughout our culture. I realize
that race and racism are not living organisms. But they have,
besides an impersonal, institutional form, a quality of fretful
aliveness, an active agency. For instance, terms like "enlightened" and "subtle" racism have been used to describe one
transformation of racism: the shift from overt racism to
covert forms that thrive on codes, signals, and symbols.

The "race card" metaphor is a limited way to understand
how race operates. It fails to show how racism poisons civic
life and denies the worth of human beings because of their
color. Race is a set of beliefs and behaviors shaped by culture,
rooted in history, and fueled by passions that transcend
reason.

The black-white divide has been the major artery through which the blood of bigotry has flowed throughout the body politic for most of the history of America.

———

I love black folk, which is why I ain't afraid of them. I'm not afraid to disagree with mass black opinion, to call into question beliefs, habits, dispositions, traditions, and practices that I think need to be criticized. I seek to speak truth to power in love, as the Bible suggests. I seek to address the high and low, those on the inside and those locked out. That's my obligation and lifelong objective.

———

The path of least resistance for those looking to dodge the burden of race is ignoring race. Although ignoring race is often mistaken for self-hatred, they are not the same. Those who confuse them commit what philosophers call a "category mistake." In such cases, shades of meaning slip off the edges of sloppy distinctions. Those who ignore race, and those who hate themselves because they can't, do share self-defeating habits: both deny the differences race makes and the lingering effects of racism. But not all blacks who have these habits hate themselves or consciously set out to ignore race. Some blacks are simply nonconformists who seek to defy the bitter boundaries of race, both within and beyond black life.

———

I think there is a *juvenocracy* operating in many urban homes and communities. For me, a juvenocracy is the domination of black and Latino domestic and urban life by mostly male figures under the age of twenty-five who wield considerable economic, social, and moral influence. A juvenocracy may consist of drug gangs, street crews, loosely organized groups, and individual youths who engage in illicit activity. They operate outside the moral and political bounds of traditional homes and neighborhoods. The rise of a juvenocracy represents a significant departure from home and neighborhood relations where adults are in charge. Three factors are at the heart of such a shift: the extraordinary violence of American life; an underground economy driven by crack and other drugs which shifted power to young black and Latino males in the homes and on the streets of major cities; and the rise of the culture of the gun in our country.

———

If we're going to have real progress in thinking and talking about race, we must not reduce racial issues to black and white. The tricky part is acknowledging the significant Latino, Asian, and Native American battles with whiteness that have taken place in our nation while admitting that the major race conflict has involved African Americans resisting black subordination in the war against white supremacy.

MED

chapter 13

Leadership

If we delude ourselves into believing that our
leaders, even our heroes, have not at times
fallen, we deny ourselves the powerful lessons
of their struggle for moral maturity.

Those leaders who are in touch with their own limitations often display a political prudence that matches their personal humility.

The death of American leaders and heroic figures like Abraham Lincoln, and John and Robert Kennedy, made them the subjects of national memory through eulogies and memorials, and gained them even greater status as the vehicles of American moral and social redemption.

In the magical arc of Colin Powell's triumphant patriotism, Frederick Douglass elbows Thomas Jefferson for a spot at Dwight Eisenhower's side.

There was, especially as a young black leader, a defiant swagger in Jesse Jackson, an athlete's bold self-possession: the confidence of the utterly black-and-beautiful. And with the rise of a black power esthetic that Jackson embraced, his youthful Afro was the bane of the bourgeoisie, and a sign of self-acceptance to the brothers and sisters in the streets who struggled for self-recognition. Jackson's black nationalist, and at other times, ghetto country getup — dashikis and denim in smooth sartorial rotation, and neck medallions and cowboy boots too, and turtlenecks and suede sports jackets — were the garb and accessories of his outcast spiritual shamanism. His wardrobe signified both street mesmerism and ministerial charisma, a symptom of the black working class's excommunication from privileged black circles. Jackson became an accessible icon for its grievances with black *and* white elites.

Malcolm X's name no longer belongs to him, no longer refers simply to his tall body or to his short life. Like Martin Luther King, Jr., Malcolm has come to mean more than himself. For some, Malcolm is an unreconstructed nationalist, while for others he wed his nationalist beliefs to socialist philosophy. Still others subject Malcolm to Marxist and Freudian analysis, while others emphasize his vocation as a public moralist. His stature derives as much from his detractors' exaggerated fears as from his admirers' exalted hopes. He has become a divided metaphor: for those who love him, he is a powerful lens of self-perception, a means of sharply focusing political and racial priorities; for those who loathe him, he is a distorted mirror that reflects violence and hatred.

————

Leaders who are blemish-free often possess a self-satisfaction that stifles genuine leadership.

————

Thomas Jefferson was influenced by John Locke's views on liberalism, natural rights philosophy, and enlightenment rationality, and rejected Christianity's status as revelation. Like other advocates of the enlightenment, Jefferson declared religion to be a matter of opinion. This view led him to proclaim that, should the neighbors of Americans say that there are twenty gods, or no God, such a statement would neither "break their legs or pick their pockets," precisely because it is not backed by the force of law. For Jefferson and the Founders, such an opinion is distinguished from officially established and recognized beliefs. Since the government is derived from the natural rights of human beings and not divine revelation, such opinions would neither mandate punishment nor require exceptional protection for their utterance. To act otherwise, as if the religious opinion that there was no God or that there were twenty gods could cause injury to be inflicted upon its bearer, is to acknowledge that such an utterance fractured a legally sanctioned belief about God. But this would be contrary to the constitutional view of religion.

Black leaders in the early 1900s thought their youth were just as morally wayward as the youth of our day. And many of those leaders indicted popular culture for its vicious effects on black youth. The remarkably humbling point to remember is that those youth who were seen as heading to hell in a handbasket became the grandparents and great-grandparents whose behavior is held up as the example we should aim for.

Maxine Waters's reputation draws from her bold, courageous, and relentless pursuit of justice, not only for her immediate constituents as a California congresswoman, but as a national leader of the poor, besieged, and voiceless. Whether addressing the inequities in applying the death penalty, the ongoing need for equal pay for women, or the collusion of the CIA in Contra drug trafficking in the ghetto, Waters has been unafraid to speak her mind and tell the truth. She has spent a life of dedicated service to speak for those who can't speak for themselves, a life driven by the palpable memory of deprivation, and the recall of gentle souls who didn't deserve the predicament in which they were trapped. Maxine Waters is a giant of a woman, a prophet in political dress who continues to fire our social imaginations about the wondrous possibility of helping those who can't help themselves, and thus fulfilling our highest obligation as citizens and human beings.

For many, Bill Clinton was our nation's "First Bubba," our country's "Trailer Trash Executive," our nation's "Poor White President." It tells on our bigoted cultural beliefs and social prejudices that Clinton — a Georgetown University alumnus, a Rhodes Scholar, an Oxford University and Yale University Law School graduate, and a president of the United States — could be construed in many quarters as a poor white trash, "cracker" citizen. The study of whiteness prods us to examine the means by which a highly intelligent man and gifted politician is transmuted into "Bubba" to be dismissed and demonized.

———

If we delude ourselves into believing that our leaders, even our heroes, have not at times fallen, we deny ourselves the powerful lessons of their struggle for moral maturity.

———

Black leadership across America is entangled in the thickets of a punishing irony: it is riddled by uncertainty precisely when it should be enjoying its greatest impact in our nation's history. The problem derives from changing expectations generated by increased black participation in electoral politics since the civil rights movement and concern about a transition in leadership styles.

———

James Madison, who contributed key phrases to the important Virginia Declaration of Rights, an exemplary document defending freedom of religion, proposed the language of the First Amendment that was eventually revised and enacted by the First Congress. In proposing the First Amendment, Madison was as greatly influenced by the suffering of religious dis-

senters at the hands of the Church of England as by enlightenment ideals of reason's superiority and the doctrine of natural rights. Madison argued that reason and conviction
should guide religion, and that the brutal battles over religious freedom made clear that religious belief should not be
established or imposed by the state. This was especially true
for a revealed religion like Christianity, whose claims to the
exclusive possession of truth also opened the possibility of religiously justified claims to political power. To prevent such a
prospect, Christianity had to be deprived of its potential political authority, a strategy achieved by challenging Christianity's biblical authority and claiming that it is a religion that is
governed by reason, which profoundly influenced Madison's
views of religion.

A leader need not be perfect to be useful.

There is a gender hierarchy in black churches where
women do much of the labor but are largely prevented from
the highest leadership role: the pastorate. The *ecclesiastical
apartheid* of the black church, which is more than seventy percent female, continues to reinforce the sexual inequality of
black women.

For much of our history, blacks have had to rely on
spokespersons to express our views and air our grievances to
a white majority that controlled access to everything from education to employment. For the most part, powerful whites
only wanted to see and hear a few blacks at a time, forcing us
to choose a leader — when we could. Often a leader was

selected for us by white elites. Predictably, blacks often dis-
agreed with those selections, but since the white elites had
the power and resources, their opinions counted. Such an
arrangement created tensions in black communities because
it reduced blackness to its lowest common denominator. Only
what could be condensed into speeches, editorials, and other
public declarations survived transmission to white elites.
Complexity was often sacrificed for clarity. It also made the
content of what was communicated about black culture con-
form to the spokesperson's gifts, vision, or interests. Thus, a
spokesperson had a profound impact on what goods or services the rest of his or her black constituency received. The
accountability of such leaders was often low.

Candor is rare among black leaders. Many have refrained
from public criticism of each other, for example, because of
the manipulative uses to which such criticism is often put by
white media and political opponents. But unless honest and
principled criticism of black leadership is encouraged within
black communities, an unhealthy silence will be reinforced,
tragically passing for communal loyalty and racial solidarity.

It is not hypocritical to fail to achieve the moral standards
that one believes are correct. Hypocrisy comes when leaders
conjure moral standards that they refuse to apply to themselves and when they do not accept the same consequences
they imagine for others who offend moral standards.

Colin Powell's story combines elements of racial mythology
with ideals of national character. His personal immigrant's

tale highlights and reinforces the defining features of American identity. Powell heroically turned the liabilities of race to great advantage. He conquered racism as a military hero, and in that role he shined the (often diminished) brilliance of black American life onto foreign lands and into closed minds closer to home. Powell's focus on the American dream sometimes blinds him to America's nightmares. But the general is also capable of a sober reveille: he knows the costs of denied opportunity.

Often a spokesperson for the race was selected because his themes, style, and ideology were acceptable to the white majority. Many black leaders were viewed skeptically by their constituencies. Booker T. Washington is a prime example of this model of leadership. Naturally, these conditions introduced considerable tension into the relationship between those who did the speaking and those who were spoken for. Black spokespersons acquired influence because they were given legitimacy by the white majority, whose power to establish such legitimacy was far greater than that of the black minority. As a result, those spokespersons used their power in black communities to reward loyal blacks and punish dissidents. This arrangement meant that patronage more than moral principle determined the allocation of the limited resources for which the spokesperson was a funnel. As a result, few blacks benefited from the leadership that was supposed to speak for them all.

Only recently have we had detailed histories of grass-roots leaders — often church-based women — who worked in local communities to make the black freedom struggle effective.

Though not as famous as their male counterparts, Fannie Lou Hamer, Ella Baker, Jo Ann Robinson, and Septima Clark were invaluable in helping black communities muster their moral might to resist white supremacy.

———————

Martin Luther King, Jr.'s flaws magnify his greatness because they provide a glimpse into a soul struggling with the knowledge that he was neither perfect nor pure. King's guilt about being widely celebrated, and about his own moral failures, gave him a humility that is virtually absent in contemporary leaders.

———————

His disputes with Malcolm X aside, Louis Farrakhan has proved to be a brilliant twin to the personality Malcolm shaped in the Nation of Islam. Farrakhan is one-half the fulfillment of Malcolm's divided mind about which route — separatist or limited solidarity with progressive whites — black folk should take to survive in America. If Farrakhan is Malcolm's shadow self — at least the half of Malcolm that was disdainful of white folk while he was in the Nation, and cautious about proceeding with their help once he departed — Farrakhan aggressively shields himself from Malcolm's brighter, perhaps blinding, other half. That half of Malcolm believed that caste and class should be attacked as well as race. That half of Malcolm believed that black folk should be open to socialist, humanitarian, and democratic strategies for racial uplift. That half of Malcolm believed that white folk really weren't devils. Farrakhan totes his contempt for that other side of Malcolm around his neck as a talisman. It wards off the amnesia that Farrakhan believes clouds black prophets once they go soft. It is a reminder to Farrakhan of the price black leaders pay once they lose their way in a racial wilderness where they are lured by misty dreams of cooperating with the enemy.

———

Al Sharpton's rise as a black leader in New York came at a time when there was a displacement of manufacturing jobs by the dominance of the financial, insurance, real estate, and advertising sectors. As a result, the economy shifted away from working-class workers and favored the well-trained middle- and upper-managerial classes. The New York of the '70s and '80s for black communities was marked by rising unemployment, dramatic spikes in homelessness, and vastly increased crime, driven in large part by the crack cocaine underground economy. There was also a zealous police state imposed on poor black communities, with a pronounced increase in publicized police brutality cases. This is the political and social vacuum into which Sharpton stepped to exercise his brand of leadership: an aggressive public response to the erosion of black civil rights by conjuring the parallels, and drawing distinctions, between New York and the South; linking his actions to, and patterning his public protests after, those of well-known black leaders like King and Jackson, and thus seeking to establish his pedigree and legitimacy; and protecting the black working and working poor classes from white hate mobs and a vicious police state.

———

Charismatic leadership has many virtues. One of them is the ability to inspire the masses and to dramatize the push for equality. It has vices too; charismatic leaders often don't find useful ways to transfer power or transmit authority. Lethal forms of competition are the norm more than cooperation. There are vulnerabilities and weaknesses of charismatic authority: it hinges on displacement and deceit, on vanity and viciousness, on the part of those who would carve their niche on the totem pole of black leadership. It also highlights the rule of ruthless ambition in charismatic leadership circles where the desire to point the way and be on top is a classic example of Martin Luther King's warning against the "drum major instinct." Instead of seeking to serve, the desire for premier status, to serve as "president of black America" among charismatic black leaders, fosters an intensely competitive environment fueled by *succession syndrome*.

We are plagued by either-or ethics. Some believe that morality is judged by examining the private behavior of leaders — that what one does in the bedroom is just as important as what one does in public. Others claim that private behavior has little consequence in measuring political character. The truth may lie somewhere between these extremes. Conservatives too often reduce the complexity of character to a test of sexual propriety. In assessing moral failure, they pay little attention to how political judgments may reveal ethical poverty. As long as a decision, say, to cut millions of the needy from welfare rolls is made by a politician without a sexual problem, the outrage it may cause is chalked up to ideology, not morality. On the other hand, liberals are infamous for underplaying the relation between personal and public life. When liberals justly defended Bill Clinton during the impeachment debacle, few remembered that the same president had demanded Surgeon General Joycelyn Elders's resignation after she suggested that masturbation should be openly discussed with young people. The obsession with sexual sin has distorted our understanding of the morality of leadership. Our leaders cannot possibly satisfy the demand for purity that some make. And neither should they try.

———

I read and watched the appalling discourtesy that blanketed Congresswoman Barbara Lee in the press — and the demeaning assaults on her reputation as well — all because she chose, in good conscience, to withhold her vote of support for a joint resolution of Congress authorizing the president to "use all necessary and appropriate force against those nations, organizations, or persons he determines planned, authorized, committed, or aided the terrorist attacks on September 11, 2001." While Lee listened to her conscience, others, even in her own Party, found it difficult to heed her wise words and action. Still, her convictions governed her vote — a gesture that defied unregulated political power and defended principled pacifism. But the truth is that black women like Barbara Lee have for centuries blessed our race and nation with wisdom, compassion, and moral vision. But too often, we have punished them for their prophetic insight, and ignored their gifts to our peril.

———

Our leaders will occasionally disappoint themselves and us. If we demand that they be perfect, we risk disillusionment when their shortcomings surface. The underlying flaw of our unwritten compact with leaders is the desperate need to believe that they must be pure to be effective. The best leaders concede their flawed humanity even as they aspire to lofty goals.

———

Mary Church Terrell enjoyed a distinguished career as a clubwoman, educator, writer, lecturer, and social activist for over sixty years. Terrell's social activism was jump-started in 1892 by the tragic death of her friend Thomas Moss at the hands of a white lynch mob enraged by his success as a grocer in her native Memphis. Mary Church Terrell and Frederick Douglass met with President Benjamin Harrison in the aftermath of Moss's lynching to complain of the rise of racial violence. The same year, she also became the leader of the Colored Women's League, and subsequently, in 1896, the first president of the NACW (National Association of Colored Women). For Terrell and her fellow NACW members, the fight against racism and the uplift of black women went hand in hand.

Not even Terrell's advanced age slowed her civil rights activism. When she was eighty-six years old, Terrell, who was born in 1863, led two other blacks and a white to request service at a segregated Washington, D.C., restaurant. They filed suit when the owner refused to offer them service. Eventually the case went to the Supreme Court. In the meantime, Terrell helped to boycott, picket, and sit-in at several other Washington, D.C., eateries. A year later, on July 24, Terrell died, just two weeks before the Supreme Court outlawed segregated public schools in *Brown v. Board of Education* and one year before Rosa Parks sparked the Montgomery bus boycott. Her courage and commitment to black freedom and women's rights provided a strong example of leadership.

––––––––

As the most gifted and vigilant black leader in the post-King era, Jesse Jackson has helped to guide black America through cycles of white backlash, the assertion of black power, the institutionalization and attack on affirmative action, Reagan-

ism, post–civil rights racial politics, the social and racial consequences of crack, the age of hip hop, and bitter black class
warfare. Jackson's two presidential races, in 1984 and 1988,
altered the black political landscape. Jackson garnered 3.5
million voters in his first run for the White House, and more
than doubled that number in 1988. His efforts registered massive numbers of black citizens and mobilized progressives
across the country. Jackson founded the National Rainbow
Coalition in 1984 to forge connections among various racial
and ethnic groups with an eye to transforming the American
political scene. Jackson also expanded his freedom efforts
globally, winning the release of hostages and political prison-
ers from Kuwait and Cuba. Jackson has been a relentless
force in the media, brilliantly leveraging his celebrity to explore on television and radio complex ideas, while advocating
for social change.

———————

Barack Obama must sort through three models of leadership in dealing with race. The first model of leadership is one
that transcends race. In one version of race transcending leadership, key features of the racial situation are suppressed. The
nation's past is largely ignored. Although this option is seductive, it is ultimately one that will not serve Obama or the nation well. Such an approach is based on a willful amnesia
about race that is too steep a price to pay in order to reach
what is essentially a false racial peace, an empty racial accord.
The second model is one that translates race. In this model of
leadership, all the significant features of the social order are
spoken in the language of race, are translated into the idiom
of color. This model is too narrow because it reduces the complex social strata to its racial dimensions, while other compelling features of the social order are slighted, ignored, or

erased. This model compensates the failure to consider race with the equally flawed approach of only considering race. Finally there is leadership that transforms race. In this model, a compelling account of racial facts and history is joined to an expression of what race can and should be. This model offers Obama the greatest intellectual and political freedom to explore the history of race while transforming its meaning in the future. Race transforming leadership does three good things: acknowledges racial facts and history, challenges racial orthodoxies, and links anti-racist struggle to other forms of political struggle.

――――――

Martin Luther King, Jr., is, arguably, the greatest American ever produced on our native soil. Figures like Abraham Lincoln and Thomas Jefferson seized the national imagination while holding public office. By contrast, King helped to redefine our country's destiny as a private citizen in a remarkable career that lasted a mere thirteen years. As a religious activist and social prophet, King challenged our nation's moral memory. He bid America to make good on promises of justice and freedom for all persons, promises that had been extended almost two centuries before. Part of King's enormous genius was the ability to force America to confront its conscience. He also brilliantly urged America to reclaim a heritage of democracy buried beneath cold documents and callous deeds.

Martin Luther King, Jr., is the defining American of our national history. His social vision at its best captured the deepest desire for freedom that any American has ever expressed. King's quest for true democracy is as great a pilgrimage as any American has undertaken. His hunger for real equality is as stirring a hope for national stability as any American has ever harbored. His thirst for racial redemption is as pure a faith in human morality as any American has dared to embrace. King's surrender of his life to the principles he cherished is as profound an investment in the worth of American ideals as any American ever made. King's career, with all of its flaws and failures, is simply the most faithful measure of American identity and national citizenship we are likely to witness.

MED

chapter 14

Hip Hop and Youth Culture

A lot of things in early hip hop were like
chitlins — the stuff that was largely cast away,
but then poor folk took hold of it and made it
a dynamic part of the musical diet.

Jazz was the rap of its time.

———

Artists like KRS-1 and Boogie Down Productions, Public Enemy, X-Clan, A Tribe Called Quest — and more recently 2Pac, Talib Kweli, Common, Mos Def, Bahamadia, Lauryn Hill, The Coup, Dead Prez, and Nas — have infused their art with political awareness. They have also occasionally linked their work to quests for social justice, whether making a song to galvanize social response to police brutality or to dramatize and inspire social outrage against an unjust war. At the height of politically conscious rap, during hip hop's golden age, groups like Public Enemy depended on a kind of racial and political literacy for folk to grasp what they were saying.

———

The hip hop notion that if you ain't poor and black you ain't authentic may have been generated by folk outside of the ghetto. A lot of people in the ghetto are trying to get the hell up out of there. They don't want to romanticize it. So it's not the ghetto that's being romanticized — its physical geography — so much as the intellectual attachment and intimacy that it breeds, a bond established among those who suffer and struggle together, who long for an exit from its horrible limits.

———

Many of these young hip hoppers certainly need to be talked to, and talked about, but more importantly, we should listen to them. Because the messages that they often put in our faces — messages that we don't want to hear because they make us uncomfortable — are messages that we need to hear. The political process can only be enhanced; the American democratic project can only be strengthened; and the citizenship of America can only be deepened with a profound engagement with some of the most serious problems that these young people represent — and tell us about.

———

Hip hop took root in a culture of hardship. Even the technology that played such a crucial role in rap's origins derived from hardship. Many black and brown kids in vocational school were sent to work repairing the turntables for rich suburban school kids. But that circumstance drove their experimentation with various technologies to expand hip hop's aesthetic base. So these young folk ended up putting turntables next to each other, and out of that emerged the practice of cuing up one record while the other one is playing, and you're listening to it, finding the exact spot to extend and repeat the break beat through scratching, and eventually with looping.

———

A lot of things in early hip hop were like chitlins — the stuff that was largely cast away, but then poor folk took hold of it and made it a dynamic part of the musical diet. That survival habit — of turning pork bellies into desirable menu items and eventually big business as commodities on the futures market — grew out of a culture of political and social suffering. It reminds us that politics is not only what we hear in hip hop lyrics, but it's also in the aesthetic and technical forms that derive from the cultural and intellectual imperatives of restless black innovation.

———

Hip hop needs to be called out for its lesser qualities, for its abysmal failures. But hip hop's critics ignore how some of the sharpest criticism comes from within hip hop's borders.

_____

It's a mistake for folk who are singing or rapping about political matters — as important as that is, especially in our era when traditional politics is a hard sell to youth — to believe that what they're doing is a substitute for social struggle and political engagement.

_____

It's rare that female artists in hip hop are able to express an alternative worldview where their ideas, interests, and agendas are taken seriously.

_____

By denying its musical and artistic merit, hip hop's critics get to have it both ways: they can deny the legitimate artistic standing of rap while seizing on its pervasive influence as an art form to prove what a terrible effect it has on youth.

_____

The limited success that women have enjoyed in hip hop — as lawyers, managers, and of course some record executives — should challenge the narrow roles imagined for women by some of its lyricists and rhetoricians. This stuff didn't start with hip hop; the reality is that patriarchy and sexism and misogyny are tired-and-true American traditions from which hip hop derives its understanding of how men and women should behave, and what roles they should play. But these ancient forms of sexism, patriarchy, misogyny, and femiphobia that shape the personal, and business, relationships between men and women in hip hop culture are rarely brought into view when the focus is young black folk.

_____

Many hip hop critics end up wearing their feelings on their peeves.

———

The same black youth culture that is frowned on for allegedly glamorizing dull thought — an allegation not hard to prove in the sort of hip hop obsessed with materialism, machismo, and misogyny — has also made a hero out of a fallen poet who made deep thinking sexy. His calling card consisted of politics, history, and race as much as it did raunchy boudoir talk. And given the sheer volume of Tupac's posthumous output, and the growing catalog of books about him — there are already more than a dozen in the marketplace ranging from pictorials to academic treatises — Tupac's lyrical and literary immortality are secure.

———

The DJ commands a pair of phonograph turntables. Among other functions, the DJ plays fragments of records through a technique called scratching: manually rotating a record in sharp, brief bursts of back and forth rhythmic movement over isolated portions of a song producing a scratching sound.

———

There are lyrics contained in the songs of the great Jelly Roll Morton that would make Snoop Dogg wince in embarrassment. You can read Morton's lyrics in their most distinguished place of storage, the Library of Congress. Does this mean that that august institution will one day house the Dogg's Magnum Snoopus, "Doggystyle," for future generations to lap up or howl at?

———

Its critics often fail to acknowledge that hip hop is neither sociological commentary nor political criticism, though it may certainly function in these modes through its artists' lyrics. Hip hop is still fundamentally an art form that traffics in hyperbole, parody, kitsch, dramatic license, double entendres, signification, and other literary and artistic conventions to get its point across.

———

The fact that three of the most gifted rappers come from highly educated mothers — Dr. Brenda Green is Talib Kweli's mother, the late Dr. Donda West was Kanye West's mother, and Dr. Mahalia Ann Hines is Common's mother — doesn't detract from their authenticity in my mind. Perhaps the opportunity that flowed from their lower-middle-class existence gave them perspective on the horrors they witnessed. None of these geniuses were by any means rich, so they were close enough to the ghetto to narrate the truth of what they witnessed, and maybe even lived.

———

I'm not suggesting we can't be critically engaged with our children's aesthetic expression. But how can we be effectively engaged if we don't know what we're engaging with? We don't have to romanticize our young rhetorical artists to appreciate them. Our moral traditions may lead us to repudiate most of what the worst of them do while applauding much of what the best of them do. The problem is we don't know how to make those distinctions, and a large part of not knowing how is bound up with our ethical aversion to the style these rhetoricians adopt. There's a way to be seriously critical — after all, folk who know and love hip hop manage to do it —

and still appreciate the sheer magnitude of talent that characterizes the best of pavement poetry.

———

Maybe hip hoppers wouldn't talk so much about material things if we helped give them a sense of meaning, and a means to connect to sustaining spiritual and moral and intellectual traditions. We can't hypocritically condemn the younger generation for their bling and their materialism, especially since those are staples of American culture. Money is critical to having a good life in our society. But we want to teach young folk that one can't reduce the good life to the shape of a car or the size of a house.

———

It's unfair to charge hip hop with a political failure that it was not accountable for to begin with. That's like holding Curtis Mayfield, who sang "Keep on Pushin'," accountable for the failure of the late-phase, Northern-based arm of the civil rights movement in the late 1960s, or holding James Brown, who sang "I'm Black and I'm Proud," responsible for the failure of the black power struggle in the early 1970s.

———

When hip hop started, the DJ had control and rocked the party through his sonic play and technical experimentalism. Look how it happened on the ground: what was essentially an attempt to repair broken turntables was used to generate an alternative sonic culture full of technological innovation that supposedly ignorant black and brown folk have now turned into a billion-dollar industry. Anthropologists call it *bricolage*, a French term first used by Claude Lévi-Strauss to mean using what is literally at hand to create something — a style, an approach, a practice. So these young black and brown folk took the technological leftovers of a richer consumer culture and fashioned a cultural and musical expression that has lasted to this day.

Hip hop captures the bigotry toward women, and gays and lesbians, found in the larger society — but on steroids, so to speak. It's the ugly exaggeration of viewpoints that are taken for granted in many conservative circles across the nation.

Like hip hop, jazz has a history of cultural attack. That history has been buried under an avalanche of nostalgia that hides jazz's grittier roots. For instance, during the Jazz Age and the Harlem Renaissance, the response to jazz by a large segment of the black bourgeoisie, black intellectuals, and black artists anticipated the attack on rap. Such responses reflected, and were partly driven by, the negative response to jazz of large segments of white society. Jazz was viewed as a cultural and artistic form that compromised decency and morality. It was linked to licentious behavior and lewd artistic gestures. With its "jungle rhythms," its blues base, its double entendre lyrics, and its sexually aggressive dancing, jazz, like hip hop today, was the most widely reviled music of the 1920s and '30s.

Hip hoppers joined pleasure and rage while turning the details of their difficult lives into craft and capital. This is the world hip hop would come to "represent": privileged persons speaking for less visible or vocal peers. At their best, rappers shape the tortuous twists of fate into lyrical elegies. They represent lives swallowed by too little love or opportunity. They represent themselves and their peers with aggrandizing anthems that boast of their ingenuity and luck in surviving.

Had more support been given to so-called positive hip hoppers and to revolutionary rappers who detested body bags and beer bottles; who encouraged black men to "be a father to your child"; who advocated love and respect for black women; who sought to build black communities; and who encouraged youth to study black history, the gangsta rap tide might have been stemmed. At the least, gangsta rappers might have been forced to take the internal criticisms of their hip hop peers more seriously because such criticisms would have had moral and economic support. After all, it's easier to get an album made if you're "pimpin' hoes," "cockin' glocks," or generally bitch-baiting your way through yet another tired tale about how terrible it was to come up in the hood without your father while blaming your mama for the sorry job she did than if you're promoting radical black unity or the overthrow of white racism.

The MC, or rapper, recites lyrics in a rhythmic, syncopated fashion. The rapper's rhetorical quirks, vocal tics, rhyme flow, and verbal flourishes mark his or her individual style. In the early days of rap, MCs often simulated sonic fragments with their voices, causing some rappers to be dubbed human beat boxes. Rappers can use a variety of rhyme schemes, from couplets in tetrameter to iambic pentameter. Their rhyme schemes can employ masculine and feminine rhymes, assonantal and consonantal rhymes, or even internal rhymes. Rappers may use enjambment, prosody, and sophisticated syncopations to tie their collage of rhymes into a pleasing sonic ensemble.

While it's easy to see why hip hop is deemed a postmodern art form — quotation, pastiche, contingency, fragmentation and the like help define its presence — it may be that its homegrown nostalgia and hunger for purity and authenticity betray modernist obsessions.

A lot of real gangsters prefer Al Green to Ice T.

When my dear friends Wynton Marsalis, Stanley Crouch, and other critics perched aloft the wall of high black culture throw stones at hip hop, they forget that such stones were once thrown at their music of preference. Bebop was once hip hop. Ragtime was once rap. Bluesmen were once b-boys. What is now noble was once notorious.

Hip hop culture has come a long way since its fledgling start in the late 1970s. Early hip hoppers were largely anonymous and could barely afford the sound systems on which the genre is built. By contrast, contemporary artists reap lucrative contracts, designer clothing lines, glossy magazine spreads, fashionable awards, global recognition, and often the resentment of their hip hop elders. If there is a dominant perception about today's rap superstars among hip hop's purists, it is that they have squandered the franchise by being obsessed with shaking derrieres, platinum jewelry, fine alcohol, premium weed, pimp culture, gangster rituals, and thug life. Although hip hop has succeeded far beyond the Bronx of its birth, it has, in the minds of some of its most ardent guardians, lost its soul.

The global portrayal of black life surely cannot rest on the images or words of barely postadolescent entertainers. This is not to deny that a single video by a rap artist can more successfully shred international boundaries than a hundred books by righteous authors. Neither is it to deny the huge responsibility such artists bear in confirming or combating hateful and ignorant beliefs about black folk that circulate around the globe. But that is just it: these beliefs are part of the ancient legacies of colonialism, racism, and regionalism, legacies that persist despite the efforts of intellectuals, artists, and leaders to destroy them. Is it fair to expect DMX to achieve what W. E. B. Du Bois could not, or for Tupac to succeed where Archbishop Tutu failed? The complex relationship between art and social responsibility is evident, but we must be careful not to place unrealistic, or even unjust, demands on the backs of artists. Their extraordinary influence cannot be denied, but the very argument that is often used against them — that they are not politicians, leaders, or policymakers, just entertainers who string together lines of poetic meter — is often conveniently forgotten when it might work to hip hoppers' advantage.

Taking the time to learn what our youth are thinking and why they create the art they do demands a capacity for deferred justification that most adults lack. They seek to ensure the legitimacy of their moral critique by rendering quick and easy judgments about the art form. Many critics of hip hop do not have the ethical patience to empathize with the formi-

dable array of choices, conflicts, and dilemmas that many
poor black youth confront.

The gangsta rap genre of hip hop emerged in the late '80s
on the West Coast as crack and gangs ruled the urban centers
of Los Angeles, Long Beach, Compton, and Oakland. Since hip
hop has long turned to the black ghetto and the Latino barrio
for lyrical inspiration, it was inevitable that a form of music
that mimicked the violence on the streets would rise. Left in
the shadow of East Coast rap for years, West Coast rap rein-
vigorated the hip hop game by reinventing the premise of rap:
to groove the gluteus maximus. As Ralph Ellison said, geography is fate. West Coast hip hop tailored its fat bass beats and
silky melodies for jeeps that cruise the generous spaces of the
West, and for the open spaces of the Midwest and the South.

For the past two decades, rap artists — who as informal
chroniclers of black youth culture translate the unspoken suffering of poor black masses into articulate anger — have
warned of the genocidal consequences of ghetto life for poor
blacks. Their narratives, though plagued by vicious forms of
misogyny and homophobia that merit strong criticism, communicate the absurdity and desperation, the chronic hopelessness, which festers inside many urban areas.

The ghetto became the source root, the major metaphor,
for Tupac's art and life, and the means by which he transformed his existence. Through his fixation on the ghetto,
Tupac made sure that there was a black tint on the universal
human quest for meaning. I think in this regard about Victor

Frankl and logotherapy, or the quest for meaning in the midst of the horror and death of the Nazi concentration camps. Tupac was articulating, in a sense, a kind of ghetto logotherapy, a quest for existential wholeness in the midst of the horror of poverty, material deprivation, and social dislocation. By remaining true to exploring the specific elements of the ghetto experience, he gave it universal appeal.

———

White kids are adopting the dress, diction, and demeanor of urban black youth. From baggy pants to oversize shirts, the "gear" of hip hop culture has been mass-produced and worn by youth of every ethnic and racial group. The slang of hip hop is now widely used. The swagger of black youth, the sultry way they combine boasting and self-confidence, has influenced the styles of upper-middle-class white youth. For many white parents, however, such a trend is cause for concern. While white youth already face their version of the generation gap — they've been dubbed "slackers" and "Generation X" — emulating the styles, speech, and behavior of urban black youth is even more menacing. It wasn't until rap made a huge impact on white kids that the music was so roundly attacked. As long as the "bad" effects of rap were restricted to black kids, its menace went undetected, unprotested, or it was flat-out ignored.

———

Although widely celebrated as the East Coast's answer to the rhetoricians of glorified violence out West, Biggie Smalls could deliver brilliant social analysis and moving portraits of poverty with metaphoric wittiness and rhythmic flow, as he does on a lyric from his first album, *Ready to Die*, remembering how "the landlord dissed us / No heat, wondered why

Christmas missed us / Birthdays was the worst days / Now we sip champagne when we thirsty / Damned right I like the life I live / 'Cause I went from negative to positive." Biggie's lyrics speak directly to the question of black suffering and what's known in theological circles as "the problem of evil." Biggie shares honors with Tupac in the articulation of a grassroots secular urban theodicy.

I caught Jay-Z in concert at Madison Square Garden in May of 2008, and he weighed in on George W. Bush, and Barack Obama too. With a huge portrait of the president projected on the screen behind him, the lyrically sophisticated griot stopped the music so that his words of critique would sink in as deep as the waters that soaked the Gulf Coast during Katrina, the subject of his riveting "Minority Report." After declaring that his people "were poor before the hurricane came" the rapper defended those survivors who were demonized, by asking in a powerful couplet: "Wouldn't you loot, if you didn't have the loot? / Baby needed food and you stuck on the roof." Jay-Z observed in compelling cadence the bitter irony of how a helicopter "swooped down just to get a scoop / Through his telescopic lens but he didn't scoop you."

But the rapper reserved his most biting indictment for an indifferent "commander-in-chief who just flew by" and refused to share even the space in his plane with the suffering survivors. Jay-Z imagined what might have happened "if he ran out of jet fuel and just dropped, Huh, that woulda been something to watch / Helicopters doing fly-bys to take a couple of shots / Couple of portraits then ignored 'em, He'd be just another bush surrounded by a couple orchids / Poor kids just 'cause they were poor kids, Left 'em on they porches / Same old story in New Orleans." After asking his throng of revelers if they were ready for change — but not without offering a disclaimer that his gesture wasn't endorsed by the presidential contender — Jay-Z flashed a picture of Obama onscreen as his audience roared its approval. The rapper's partisan vibe carried the day as an interlude to his entrancing performance.

———

Unlike Ralph Ellison's character in his famous novel *Invisible Man* and the bulk of black folk for a long stretch of our history, black youth suffer, not from invisibility, but from hypervisibility. The surplus sighting, and citing, of young black bodies — in crime stories on the news, in congressional hearings about demeaning imagery in pop music, in shopping malls where they hang out, in police profiles where they are stigmatized, in suburban communities where they are surveilled — has draped paranoia and panic around their very limbs. In all the wrong ways, black youth are overexposed. Is it any wonder, then, that they dress in oversize clothing to hide their demonized bodies, to diminish the measuring of their alleged menace?

———

The producer has several devices at her command, including a beat box and digital sampler. The beat box, or drum machine, is an electronic instrument that simulates the sound of a drum set. A digital sampler is a synthesizer that stores in its computerized memory a variety of sounds (a James Brown scream, a TV theme song, a guitar riff, a bass line) that are reproduced when activated by the producer. The DJ and the producer work together in laying down backing tracks for the MC. The tracks consist of rhythms, scratches, beats, shrieks, noise, other sound effects, and loops, which are fragments of existing songs reworked and repeated in new musical contexts.

In 2005, hip hop legend Nas joined his noted musician father Olu Dara for an imaginative duet on the song "Bridging the Gap" that plunged deeply into the Delta region's distinctive musical history. From its opening blues vamp, drenched in a Bo Diddley-meets-Muddy Waters rhythmic swagger, it is clear that Nas and Olu Dara have wed two powerful art forms in exploring the area's vibrant musical tradition. By now it's a cliché for hip hoppers to join the rap-rock brigade. But there are precious few rappers who've bothered to tap the fertile sonic vein that produced rock — and hip hop as well. After all, with its double entendres, colorful language, relentless boasting, homespun machismo, and tragicomic sensibility, the blues are a forceful parent to rap. Olu Dara and Nas brilliantly play off of the kinship of their music and manhood on their powerful collaboration. "Bridging the Gap" is a soulful tribute to the roots shared by father and son, by the rural and the urban, and by two supremely gifted artists.

The best hip hop rhetoricians, in their social and artistic functions, have a great deal in common with some of the greatest rhetoricians ever. One thinks about Shakespeare or Chaucer or the writer of *The Decameron*. One thinks about Melvin Tolson, or Langston Hughes, or Nikki Giovanni, or Sonia Sanchez. One thinks about Walt Whitman. One thinks about Yeats or Rilke. One thinks about a whole range of poetic meters and inventions and rhythms and tonalities. One thinks of Yosef Koumunyakaa, Elizabeth Alexander and Jayne Cortez, or Thomas Sayers Ellis experimenting with the beat of go-go music in his poetic meter. So when you think about all this, the amazing thing is that these young rhetoricians are denied the legitimacy of their accomplishment because we pathologize them on a moral level. The moral qualms of some black folk have obscured the genius of their own children who, like jazz artists, have to go foreign before they become familiar. They have to go global before they find local appeal. We saw this with the magazines. Before they were put on black magazines they were put on white magazines. Before they were featured on BET, they were on MTV. So they had to go away before they could come home.

What these young folk in hip hop do with the language is nothing short of remarkable. They don't simply replicate what they've been given; they stretch it out, break some of it off, re-constitute it, and prove that literary critic Jacques Derrida is right, that we "only ever have one language" that is "not at one with itself." We have a plurality of voices and rhetoric, and that there's "no such thing as *a* language." We should practice linguistic humility — and not rhetorical condescension — and be mindful of our children's sheer verbal wizardry and inventiveness.

Amnesia and anger have teamed up to rob many blacks of a balanced perspective on our kids. With such balance, we might justly criticize and appreciate hip hop culture. Without the moderating influence of historical insight, joined to what might be called the humility of memory, we end up mirroring the outright repudiation our kids face across this country.

MED

chapter 15

Homosexuality and Homophobia

Are gays and lesbians who remain faithful to their partners committing a greater sin than married heterosexuals who commit adultery?

Sacred orientation is more important than sexual orientation.

———

All of us have to confront the sexism, misogyny, patriarchy, and homophobia that are so deeply rooted in our culture. I try to embrace and live by feminist principles, but I'm constantly at war with the deeply ingrained sexism of the culture that seeps into my brain. The same is true for homophobia. That's the challenge I face: to confront and reject male supremacy and heterosexist bigotry even as we together confront and reject them in the broader society.

———

We say that God took on flesh and became a human being — not an idea, not a cosmic principle, not a theory, not a political abstraction. That's why we must treat the human body with respect. All bodies deserve love and protection — gay bodies and straight ones, colored bodies and white ones, female bodies and male ones, foreign bodies and American ones, poor bodies and rich ones, imprisoned bodies and free ones. All human bodies are important because they are the product of God's imagination meeting up with human circumstance.

———

I happen to believe that gays and lesbians can no more get up tomorrow morning and be heterosexual than heterosexuals can get up tomorrow morning and be gay or lesbian.

———

The gay male upsets the social order for the straight male. Straight males want to celebrate male athletes or religious figures without fear of being charged with an erotic or sexual attraction to them. The presence of a gay male throws things off, and therefore, the straight male argues for erotic segregation, so that rigid lines can be drawn between the kind of desire that straight and gay males have. You can understand that there'd be a lot of self-questioning, self-doubting, and questioning and doubting of others, as a result of homoerotic desire invading the fortress of straight male desire.

———

Are gays and lesbians who remain faithful to their partners committing a greater sin than married heterosexuals who commit adultery?

———

We've been having a huge debate in American society about gay and lesbian marriage, and one thing we could depend upon was black and brown communities offering extraordinary support to the conservative former president Bush and his allies in their assault on the liberties and civil rights of these gay and lesbian people. Bush appealed to conservative evangelical beliefs about sexuality, and gender, and a narrow, literal reading of the Bible that appeals to a lot of blacks and Latinos. That always trips me out because I wonder how people who were illiterate less than 150 years ago could be biblical literalists! After all, the same kind of biblical literalism used to justify black oppression and enslavement is now used to justify resistance to gays and lesbians — and many black folk are in league with them. That's just tragic, and I say this as an ordained Baptist preacher rooted deeply in progressive evangelical territory.

———

Black Christians, who have been despised and oppressed for much of our existence, should be wary of extending that oppression to our lesbian sisters and gay brothers.

———

If we, as heterosexual men, see two lesbians kissing each other, not only are we not necessarily turned off, we might even be turned on. Lesbian sexuality can in some cases be tolerated, even encouraged, because it can be useful to heterosexual male desire: two for the price of one. We can swing the women our way to allow us to participate in a ménage à trois! You can imagine a brother saying, "Oh, I don't mind if you get into bed with me with your other girl because she might please us both." So there's great room in the heterosexual world for situational lesbianism that serves straight male sexuality.

———

Young black male rappers are obsessed with the terms and tensions of black manhood, often employing women and gays as rhetorical foils in exploring what they think is authentic masculinity.

———

What's intriguing to me about the tensions, and therefore, the connections, between homophobic and homoerotic men is that they both have stakes in the same body. Straight and gay men are equally invested in the same testosterone-soaked athletic contest where men are slapping each others' behinds on the basketball court, or patting each others' booties after making a touchdown. The same straight and gay males go to church and leap to their feet and vigorously proclaim, "I love him! I love him," speaking about another man — Jesus. The same actions can count as heterosexual or homoerotic. Slapping behinds, patting booties, hugging, and hollering about Jesus — all these activities count for heterosexuals and homosexuals at the same time, depending on how you interpret them.

The notorious homophobia of the black church just doesn't square with the numerous same-sex unions taking place, from the pulpit to the pew. One of the most painful scenarios of black church life is repeated Sunday after Sunday with little notice or collective outrage. A black minister will preach a sermon railing against sexual ills, especially homosexuality. At the close of the sermon, a soloist, who everybody knows is gay, will rise to perform a moving number, as the preacher extends an invitation to visitors to join the church. The soloist is, in effect, being asked to sing, and to sign, his theological death sentence. His presence at the end of such a sermon symbolizes a silent endorsement of the preacher's message. Ironically, the presence of his gay Christian body at the highest moment of worship also negates the preacher's attempt to censure his presence, to erase his body, to deny his legitimacy as a child of God. Too often, the homosexual dimension of eroticism remains cloaked in taboo or blanketed in theological attack. As a result, the black church, an institution that has been at the heart of black emancipation, refuses to unlock the oppressive closet for gays and lesbians.

Body piercing may now be seen as the body's crochet needle, allowing participants to embroider the skin in striking patterns of self-disclosure. Of course, as was true with disco music, body piercing, which thrives in gay and lesbian cultures, represents the "homosexualization" of American expressive culture while underscoring the exhibitionist impulses of consumer culture.

I often joke with my son, "If you're so interested in protecting yourself from gay men, you're giving somebody an easy shot at your butt with your pants sagging so low and your draws showing." So even in the most hallowed heterosexual circles, homoerotic bonding occurs on the regular. That's bound to cause a lot of straight guys to worry about their own sexuality, or to ask if what they're doing is pure or being contaminated with homoerotic sentiment. You can see how easily that might lead these straight men to question themselves, and therefore, direct enormous fury at gay males and gay culture. It's precisely because the meanings are shared, and sexual meanings slide easily between straight and gay male culture, that there is such huge hatred for homosexuals among heterosexual men.

Perhaps if gay and lesbian church members could come out of their closets, they could leave behind as well the destructive erotic habits that threaten their lives.

During the 2004 election, many conservative blacks voted for Bush because of his opposition to gay marriage. This political red herring diverted critical attention from Bush's failure to address the social and economic inequities that still hamper progress and equality for millions of poor blacks. This shift among black voters reinforced ugly homophobia. But it also absorbed precious cultural resources that might have relieved the suffering of the black poor instead of increasing the suffering of gay, lesbian, transgender, and bisexual brothers and sisters. The greater tragedy is that such efforts were sparked by conservative figures that have proved hostile to the interests of black folk.

As they say in Christian circles, God didn't make any junk, and that means that whomever God has made, whether homosexual or heterosexual, is a good person.

Homoerotic moments show up in hip hop in at least a couple of ways. First, when hip hop artists speak about M.O.B. — "money over bitches" — they are emphasizing the crass relation between commerce and misogyny. But there's another element to M.O.B. as well: that of placing one's "homies" above women, because men make money with men — or take money from them. In any case, the male relation becomes a fetish in hip hop circles: hanging with "my boys," kicking it with "my crew," hustling with "my mens and them," and dying for "my niggas." There is an unapologetic intensity of devotion that surely evokes homoerotic union at some level. Second, there is great exaggeration or even mythology about sexual conquests performed in the presence of one or more participating men. "I hit it, then my boy hit it," some young men brag, while others boast of multiple men having consensual sex with a woman. One assumes that males expose their sexual organs in such conquests — especially as they mimic the sexual gestures adapted from the pornographic films that are increasingly popular in certain hip hop circles. This is surely a heated and heady moment of homoerotic bonding.

There is an aggressive, and progressive, gay, lesbian, bisexual, transgender presence in black America that gains the political meaning of their identity by fighting both racism in gay communities and homophobia in black life. They challenge the monolithic conception of black identity while forging solidarity in the fight against the terrors of race and class. In the past, this group included James Baldwin, and more recently, the late Audre Lorde, and today it includes Barbara Smith, Randall Kenan, E. Lynn Harris, Keith Boykin and Meshell Ndegeocello.

The obsession in black culture with the "positive" versus the "negative" can sometimes be a problem. There's bitter disagreement about whether gay or lesbian people have a rightful spot at the table of black identity. And for people who are in black churches, it's negative to talk about homosexuality and lesbianism. And yet those are our brothers and sisters.

When black folk say "our agenda," what agenda is that? You see, black America is now so split and fractured along multiple axes. Race is a unifying fiction that still resonates in black communities and gives unity to the experiences of many individuals. But then, when you start breaking it down in subsections and subcategories and so on, when you talking about "we," black people say, "We down for unity" — until we start talkin' bout the gay folk. "Well, we got to purify them 'cause the Bible say they doin' wrong." Already you got a problem. Because no longer is it a unified "we"; it's a fractured "we." It's "we" with an asterisk — everybody *except* the gays and lesbians, transgenders, and bisexuals.

Given the history of American society in its bigotry toward gays and lesbians, we must acknowledge that we live in a heterosexist culture that privileges the viewpoints of people who happen to be "normal." Normal is defined as those of us who are heterosexual. Therefore, there is a particular kind of bigotry that is directed toward people who are gay and lesbian. It is sometimes a subspecies — that is the hatred of gays — of attempted murder and we have to have laws that deal with that.

There's no question that George W. Bush was prosecuting war on all fronts, so that cultural conflict became the war on terror by other means. What I mean, more specifically, is that all of this brouhaha occasioned by civil marriages versus gay marriages, for example, just served to ratchet up an atmosphere of paranoia which seemed to say: "You had better watch out because the terrorist that lurks outside is also the kind of cultural terrorist that looms large domestically. Those who support a gay or lesbian living next door to them are the same people who were telling this country to be critical of the Bush administration; they want to reject your evangelical Christianity or your conservative Judaism. They're now assaulting you." So I think there was a concerted ideological effort to create an environment of paranoia around cultural values and to link that cultural fear to political fear. That kind of ideological illusion is brilliant, but I think it's ultimately perverted.

Critics who seek to proof-text their opposition to homosexuality often neglect to interpret such biblical passages in their larger theological meaning. For instance, the story of Sodom and Gomorrah is more about understanding the necessity for hospitality to strangers than it is about homosexual perversion.

———————

The terror to which lesbians, gays, bisexual, and transgender citizens are vulnerable is often overlooked or scoffed at by most of us who fall outside their ranks. The religious justification for the social stigma of homosexuality — and in some cases, for the violence expressed toward gay and lesbian people — is taken for granted in many quarters of the culture. To be sure, many will claim that there is hardly a justifiable comparison between what happened on 9/11 and the oppression faced by racial, gender, and sexual minorities. And yet the same bigotry, and the violence it encourages, lay at the base of what we witnessed on 9/11 and the experience of the victims of racism, sexism, and homophobia. At its best, religion provides theological support for the most vulnerable members of our culture and argues against the violence done in God's name to all victims of terror, whether their cause is given global recognition or buried on the back pages of history. In fact, for those who suffer the latter fate, it is even more reason to link their oppression to a suffering we readily understand and acknowledge, and with which we sometimes empathize. In so doing, we meet the nearly universal moral criteria of all religious faiths: to remember victims of all terrors and to seek justice on their behalf, even if the national mood or country's self-image are challenged by our action.

———————

There's no homosexual exemption to racial self-hatred. In fact, for the black gay or lesbian, there is greater danger: with the black self and the gay self in tandem, there are more selves to despise, resent, even hate.

Despite his Hebrew Pentecostal pedigree, with its rigidly repressed views of sexuality, Marvin Gaye's father, Rev. Gay, was a flamboyant and effeminate man. He liked to dress in women's clothing and makeup. Rev. Gay's sexual ambivalence and "male femaling" — males who adopt female identities in various ways and contexts with varying results — showed in his overtly feminine speech and body language. Marvin's mother says that Rev. Gay preferred soft clothing. He also liked to dress in her panties, shoes, gowns, and nylon hose. Rev. Gay also favored colorful silk blouses and occasionally straight-hair wigs. Rev. Gay would sometimes put waves in his hair. At other times he let it grow long and curled it under. Marvin often glimpsed Rev. Gay in his "male femaled" form. Throughout Marvin's ghetto neighborhood, Rev. Gay was referred to as "sissy." Questions arose about Rev. Gay's sexuality: was he homosexual, bisexual or just weird? Neither Marvin nor his mother knew for certain. But Rev. Gay loved beautiful women with large buttocks and breasts. He is rumored to have had several girlfriends. He exploited his pastoral position to draw "sisters" at church to his bed.

The great R&B artist Leon Ware thinks that only the profoundly insecure have to wage war to defend their religious beliefs. Likewise, he thinks the same insecurity haunts heterosexual men who are unnerved by gay men. For Ware, the bottom line is mutual respect and a sense of love that flows from our sensual recognition of the other.

Unfortunately, differences within black life have been viewed by many leaders and intellectuals as signs of our surrender to the corrupting influence of the white world. On this view, homosexuality is for white folk, a perversion they invented because they had too much leisure time gained in pillaging and plundering non-white peoples. Not only is being a "fag" or a "dyke" downright unnatural, such logic goes, but it misrepresents sexual traditions of black American society, and before that, African culture. To believe that, you've got to overlook the brilliant contributions and sexual habits of Alain Locke and James Baldwin, or Bessie Smith and Audre Lorde. The differences that these differences make within black culture are too important to simply be dismissed.

The force of class, the role of gender, and the rise of gay sexuality to prominence in our culture cautions against seeing race as the only lodestar of identity. These mixtures also challenge simple analyses of oppression that fail to grasp the creolized character of American identity.

I am wholly sympathetic to sharp criticism of gangsta rap's sexism and homophobia, though most of the critics of hip hop's bitterness toward women have made little of the latter plague. "Fags" and "dykes" are prominent in the genre's vocabulary of rage. Critics' failure to make this an issue only reinforces the inferior, invisible status of gay men and lesbians in mainstream and black life. Homophobia is a vicious emotion and practice that links mainstream black institutions to the vulgar expressions of gangsta rap. There seems to be an implicit agreement between gangsta rappers and political

elites that gays, lesbians, and bisexuals basically deserve what
they get.

———————

One of the most vicious effects of the closet is that some of
the loudest protesters against gays and lesbians in the church
are secretly homosexual. In fact, many, many preachers who
rail against homosexuality are themselves gay. Much like the
anti-Semitic Jew, the homophobic gay or lesbian Christian se-
cures his or her legitimacy in the church by denouncing the
group of which he or she is a member, in this case an almost
universally despised sexual identity. On the surface, such an
act of self-hatred is easy. But it comes at a high cost. Homophobic rituals of self-hatred alienate the gay or lesbian believer from his or her body in an ugly version of erotic
Cartesianism: splitting the religious mind from the homosexual body as a condition of Christian identity. This erotic Cartesianism is encouraged when Christians mindlessly repeat
about gays and lesbians, "we love the sinner but we hate the
sin." A rough translation is "we love you but we hate what you
do." Well, that mantra worked with racists: we could despise
what racist whites did while refusing to despise white folk
themselves, or whiteness per se. But with gay and lesbian
identity, to hate what they do is to hate who they are. Gays
and lesbians are how they have sex. I'm certainly not reducing
gay or lesbian identity to sexual acts. I'm simply suggesting
that the sign of homosexual difference, and hence the basis
of their social identification, is tied to the role of the sex act,
or the desire for it, in their lives.

———————

The coming-out process is often especially volatile: it involves the painful irony of self-identification with the very sex-

ual identity that has been culturally demonized. That's why there's so much self-hatred among gays and lesbians.

One of the most crucial issues a liberating interpretation of the Bible can address is the culture of dishonesty that smothers homosexuals. Gays and lesbians often have had to deny to themselves they were homosexual. They denied their sexuality to others who might have perceived it even before they did, a perception that might have caused them great discomfort. They often have had to stay in a theological closet, and to some degree, a biological closet, because they didn't want to suffer the consequences of coming out. The culture of deceit imposed on gays and lesbians has to be relieved by the church's open affirmation of their legitimacy, so that they don't have a distorted consciousness and a bruised conscience about their own sexuality. In the final analysis, we are liberated into self-acceptance by a loving and forgiving God.

I'm not suggesting that white gays and lesbians cannot be white supremacists, or that they cannot derive benefits, pleasures, and perks from white skin privilege. In fact, their white supremacist fantasies can be projected onto black bodies. For instance, the well-endowed black male can be ravenously sought by gay white men who possess stereotypical views of black sexuality, aping the behavior of some white straight communities. Still, I must add, without generalizing them, that white gays and lesbians seem more aware as a group of the complex racial dynamics of personal and social relations than their straight counterparts. That's just an informal observation about how one minority is sometimes sensitive to the plight of another minority — although we know the opposite is also true, since there's plenty of ignorance and big-otry to go around in straight black communities and in gay and lesbian white communities.

We don't have to stop being black to be saved. We don't have to stop being women to be saved. We don't have to stop being poor to be saved. And we don't have to stop being gay or lesbian to be saved.

MED

chapter 16

Poverty and Class

We should love the poor and hate poverty.

God came to earth to die as one of the poor and outcast.

The poor are, in effect, socially dead persons. They suffer social alienation: they lack standing, status, and protection; they are mercilessly flogged in the press, demonized by fellow citizens, made a football by politicians, viciously criticized by public policy makers, and assaulted by scholars and intellectuals. The stigma the poor carry bans them from the presumption of political innocence, of being good citizens; they carry the weight of social pariah. They walk in the door with a capital "P" on their foreheads.

People who give money to the poor deserve praise; people who give their lives to the poor deserve honor.

Whether black folk have set foot in the Promised Land, or got lost in the wilderness, depends on whom you ask and what you see. Quarters of black America have boomed into the upper reaches of prosperity. The wealthiest black folk, and the merely rich, have fared very well, more annoyed than trumped by racial beliefs and barriers. Due in large part to affirmative action, the upper-middle classes continue to rise, but their arc of triumph sometimes dead-ends in ceilings lowered on their professional ambitions, in particular for black women. The lower-middle and middle-middle classes are struggling but, to varying degrees, maintaining. The lower classes, meanwhile, are suffering greatly. The working poor are barely surviving, while the black impoverished — variously called the permanently poor, the ghetto poor, the underclass, or the "outer class" because they are banished to the outskirts of prosperity and respect — are struggling against the odds to eek out a living.

———————

We should love the poor and hate poverty.

———————

We can abide the ugly presence of poverty so long as it doesn't interrupt the natural flow of things, doesn't rudely impinge on our daily lives or awareness. As long as poverty is a latent reality, a solemn social fact suppressed from prominence on our moral compass, we can find our bearings without fretting too much about its awkward persistence.

———————

In America we can be affluent in any language.

———————

The black poor have been made a political piñata: public policy makers, politicians, and cultural critics of varying stripes blindfold themselves to the dignity and humanity of the poor to strike at them with vicious stereotypes, and often hardened hearts, savoring from their broken images the sweet but soulless satisfaction of defeating the already defeated.

———————

Although the black middle class has boomed, and is a more sophisticated and complex population than suggested by E. Franklin Frazier's portrait of paranoia and insecurity, it lacks the resources to pull the vast majority of blacks into its precincts of privilege.

———————

When my pregnant wife, Terrie, and I were kicked out of
our apartment on Christmas Day, things got far worse before
they got better. We found a vacant flat to rent, but it hardly
felt like home — the man with whom we shared the bathroom
pulled a pistol on me. Squirrels regularly scurried in and out
of a hole in the wall of our unit. We were often too poor to eat
every day, although occasionally a friend from church would
leave groceries on our steps. Terrie eventually had to give up
her job as a waitress when she started to show — she had one
of those jobs where the waitresses wore hot pants and tiny
tops — and I was eventually fired from my clerk's job at
Chrysler that my wife's uncle helped me to secure (an unjust
firing, I might add, as I'll never forget my boss's words, "It had
to be somebody's ass, and I'd rather it be yours than mine.")
We were forced to live on welfare, since I lost my job a little
more than a month before my son was born. We got food
stamps and government medical assistance to pay the costs
of delivering our baby. My wife was enrolled in W.I.C.
(Women, Infants and Children), and I stood many a day in
those long lines and collected packets of powdered milk and
artificial eggs — just as I stood in line at the welfare office,
where the civil servants were often rude and loud, making the
experience that much more degrading.

If racism is destroyed tomorrow, many blacks and Latinos
who are poor will still be poor.

While others made war on the poor, Martin Luther King
made war on what made them poor. He moved in 1966 into a
Chicago slum for several months to dramatize the plight of
the poor, and to put flesh to the spirit of nonviolent resistance

to "the violence of poverty." At the urging of activist Marian Wright Edelman, King began the Poor People's Campaign to bring national attention to the poor of all races. He joined with a coalition of activists across the racial and ethnic spectrum to fight poverty in a planned march on Washington, D.C., in April of 1968. It was the first stage of a massive; aggressively nonviolent movement that called on poor people and their allies to take up residence in the nation's capital for months and, if necessary, to shut down traffic. At the invitation of nonviolent apostle and activist James Lawson, King journeyed to Memphis to march and protest the mistreatment of poor sanitation workers on strike for better wages and just treatment. Before he was murdered, King planned to disobey a court injunction against marching to dramatize these poor black workers' plight.

We're still in the closet about class in America.

By 1993 opportunity had blossomed but so had despondency. The black upper class soared, the middle class rose, then dipped, and the black lower class sunk so low that its children were killing each other over scraps of imagined nothingness. Never before had America seen such a chasm between rich and poor, a disparity that was amplified in the blight of inner-city blacks as they were forced to watch the explosive wealth of their upper-crust brethren fail to drop the crumbs of prosperity down from their banquet tables.

It was the policies put in place by President Franklin Delano Roosevelt which first lifted many blacks out of poverty by creating programs that would today be labeled "workfare." And though these programs were not specifically designed with blacks in mind, it would be the poorest Americans who benefited most — and most of the poorest were black. The New Deal brought relief to the rural poor and funneled money into communities to create jobs, not handouts. Ironically, it would also be some of these same programs that would disenfranchise the already working poor, in particular sharecroppers, tenants, and farm laborers, none of whom were provided for in the Agricultural Adjustment Act of 1933. This particular piece of legislation would ultimately lay the groundwork for the kinds of farm subsidies that would eventually undermine the small family farm and drive even more poor rural blacks into urban environments in search of unskilled factory jobs. And it would be in the urban environment, where black parents were working numerous low-paying shifts to keep their small households afloat, that largely unchecked black youths would eventually turn to and on each other.

———

A bitter civil war waged from the inside bloodies black America. Among the greatest casualties are typically the defenseless poor. They are further disgraced by the neglect, or indifference, of their more fortunate kin. Well-positioned critics in the ruling black class snipe at the poor at the same time as they offer amnesty to their mainstream enemies. When staunchly conservative social critics witness the black fortunate lambasting their poorer brothers and sisters, it offers insurance against the charge of racial insensitivity. After all, if well-heeled blacks are harshly judging them, how can whites who make similar comments be accused of indifference to the black poor? The bitter criticisms of the black elite also embolden radical conservatives to take similarly hard-line stances that oppose social and political help for the most vulnerable. And the poor are wounded by friendly fire; even the poor learn to loathe themselves and attack other poor people.

The black working class has been literally squeezed out of its living spaces by gentrification in the inner city, where structures are overtaken by individuals and businesses with the means to rehabilitate marginal housing.

The New Deal showed blacks that they could have a place at the table, even as that table was being burned along with their churches. By funneling some poor blacks into work and others into relief situations, Roosevelt's brilliant solution to the Depression created a definable schism within black culture whose repercussions are felt to this day.

The gulf in black and white incomes is the monetary residue of inequality; it shows just how stubborn and systematic has been the denial of literal and symbolic capital to black kin. Greater education significantly boosts the odds of black folk getting bigger paychecks and more job security. For the working poor, that security all but vanishes into a haze of piecemeal jobs, part-time work, no benefits, sporadic rewards, and depressed wages — and hence, depressing prospects. The desire to work is large, the absence of sustaining work even larger.

The few resources that exist barely make it to the next black generation. The subprime mortgage crisis will cost black folk between $71 billion and $122 billion, the greatest loss of black wealth in history. Only 17.2 percent of whites have high cost loans; for blacks, the number is an astonishing 54.7 percent. The parental lift up the ladder of status is missing several rungs — gaps that accumulate as the arithmetic of negative calculation of all the goods and perks that go missing for black families, but which more well-positioned families take for granted. It is the tendency to see as natural what has been gained at someone else's expense — one's parents or grand-parents, or other sources of both rightful and unjust inheri-tance — that often turns the beneficiaries of unearned privilege so harshly against the unfortunate.

Black folk from lower economic groups are less likely to reach old age than members of other racial and ethnic groups, and those from higher income brackets.

Rich black folk are not the same as poor black folk. We are positioned differently in American culture, with different re-sources to combat our suffering. We even have different re-sources to be able to name what ails us.

Unspoken, and therefore, unresolved racial conflicts invite bad eating habits and obesity, which are in turn enabled by a shrewdly specific marketing agenda. What could possibly be right about a Styrofoam bowl filled with bits of fried chicken, mashed potatoes, corn, and cheese, smothered in gravy and held out in black hands to black customers? At 740 delicious calories (half of those from the fat content of the meal) and 2,350 milligrams of sodium — 98 percent of the recommended daily allowance — is it any wonder that poor people, who can more easily afford this conveniently packaged and priced food than fresh meats and vegetables, are steadily becoming the most obese among us?

―――――

We are perhaps the only country in the world where the rich get thinner and the poor get fatter.

―――――

The lot of millions of poor folk is to endure the gulf between hope and heartbreak.

―――――

The life of poor black folk is caught between crime and punishment. Most critics argue that those of us who beg for rationality and clarity, and for consistency and fairness, in the criminal justice system are seeking amnesty for all black criminals, or an escape of responsibility for misbehavior. Neither is true. Criminals should be held accountable for their crimes. The practice of murder to resolve conflicts has ravaged too many poor communities and must be opposed with every bit of our strength. We must preach against it, legislate against it, and march against it; but we must also demand an end to the economic and social ills that make murder a convenient tool to express aggression and secure goods in a perverted moral outlook — largely at the expense of other poor people.

―――――

The attempt to make poor blacks better has recently made some rich blacks bitter.

―――――

Homicide is often the payoff for impoverished conditions; it is the unsubtle and undisciplined hatred of the other-who-is-like-me that blooms in the psyches of those who hate themselves and their plight even more.

During the Reagan era, economic suffering drove poor black and brown youth to create something important out of the fragments of culture. It was during this time that resources were sparse, especially in cash-poor inner-city schools which endured cruel budget cuts that depleted arts programs and denied poor children access to instruments and broad musical literacy. So when older folk, especially musicians, complain that young folk don't play instruments, they must realize that there's hardly support for young folk learning to play the saxophone, or the clarinet, or the trumpet, or the drums, because those are aesthetic artifacts of a bygone musical era when the opportunity to deepen one's musical vocabulary was far greater. But economic deprivation forced poor black and brown kids into greater strategies of survival and aesthetic creativity through rap music, graffiti, and break dancing.

There's a vibrant tradition of artists — whether in the Black Arts Movement, or in the Harlem Renaissance before it with figures like Langston Hughes and Zora Neale Hurston — who helped us become more aware of, and to struggle with, the problems of the "folk" and of the poor. Their art helped black folk to identify, and to cope with, the social misery of African American people.

The burden of trying to feed mouths, and a ravenous appetite for somebodyness, can eat one's soul into depression and suicide.

———

With crack's rise, poor black and Latino communities were besieged by drug gangs, increased crime, and police surveillance and crackdowns. Besides the fact that poor black and brown communities were flooded with a cheap but lethally addictive form of cocaine, there was the problem of easy access to automatic weapons. Thus, the crack epidemic fostered the rise of violent figures that hijacked black urban America and brought considerable personal terror and domestic trauma in their wake. It also made poor black folk slaves to high-risk diversionary pleasure as a means of psychic survival, discouraging them from directly confronting the social dislocation, and the lethargy and listlessness, which the crack epidemic only made worse.

———

Politics bleed beyond narrow definitions, and thus, when rappers argue over scarce resources for their poor brothers and sisters, and question why poor black folk don't share in the economic and social bounty of mainstream America, they are behaving politically.

———

After I got Terrie pregnant at eighteen and married her, and after our son Mike was born, Daddy and I grew much closer. In fact, he'd often cook for me and Terrie because we were so poor at times that we didn't eat every day. In fact, at times, we didn't eat for two or three days in a row.

———

It's not as if it was news to most folk that poverty
the United States. Still, there was no shortage of eureka ι.
ments glistening with discovery and surprise in the aftermath
of Hurricane Katrina. Poverty's grinding malevolence is fed
in part by social choices and public policy decisions that directly impact how many people are poor and how long they
remain that way. To acknowledge that is to own up to our role
in the misery of the poor — be it the politicians we vote for
who cut programs aimed at helping the economically vulnerable; the story of bootstrap individualism we tell while ignoring the considerable benefits we've received as we bitterly
complain of the few breaks the poor might get; the religious
idea we cling to that the poor are poor because they aren't
hungry enough for prosperity; and the resentment of the alleged pathology of poor blacks, fueled more by stereotypes
than empirical support, which gives us license to dismiss or
demonize them.

Concentrated poverty — where folk live in poor neighborhoods, attend poor schools, and have poor-paying jobs that
reflect and reinforce a distressing pattern of rigid segregation
— is the product of decades of public policies and political
measures. For instance, the federal government's decision to
concentrate public housing in segregated inner-city neighborhoods fueled metropolitan expansion. It also cut the poor off
from decent housing and educational and economic opportunities by keeping affordable housing for poor minorities out
of surrounding suburbs. The effects of concentrated poverty
have been amply documented: reduced private-sector investment and local job opportunities; higher prices for the poor
in inner-city businesses; increased levels of crime; negative
consequences on the mental and physical health of the poor;

and the spatial dislocation of the poor spurred by the "black track" of middle-class households to the suburbs.

Concentrated poverty does more than undermine academic success and good health; since there is a strong relationship between education and employment, and quality of life, it keeps the poor from better paying jobs that might interrupt a vicious cycle of poverty.

Katrina's violent winds and killing waters have swept into the mainstream a stark realization: the poor had been abandoned by society and its institutions, and sometimes by their well-off brothers and sisters, long before the storm.

Lots of well-to-do black folk are doing a lot to help, but too many of us have left the black poor stranded on islands of social isolation and class alienation.

What made Kanye West's defense of the black poor so admirable is that it suggested the willingness of a rich black celebrity to sacrifice his reputation, perhaps even his livelihood, and surely his comfort, to speak out on behalf of his less-fortunate brothers and sisters.

Some of the black aristocracy in the early twentieth century used newspapers and pulpits to whip the black poor into order, to shame them, if they could, into acting right, which often meant acting white.

Our being surprised, and disgusted, by the poverty that Katrina revealed is a way of remaining deliberately naïve about the poor while dodging the responsibility that knowledge of their lives might bring. We remain ignorant of their circumstances to avoid the indictment of our consciences. When a disaster like Katrina strikes — a *natural* disaster not caused by human failure — it frees us to be aware of, and angered by, the catastrophe. After all, it doesn't directly implicate us; it was an act of God. Even when human hands get involved, our fingerprints are nowhere to be found. We're not responsible for the poor and black being left behind; the local, state, or federal government is at fault. We are thus able to decry the plight of the poor while assuring ourselves that we had nothing to do with it. We can even take special delight in lashing out at the source of their suffering — as long as it's not us. We are fine as long as we place time limits on the origins of the poor's plight — their poverty dates from the moments we all spied it on television after the storm, but not the years before when we all looked the other way. Thus we fail to confront our role in their long-term suffering. By being outraged, we appear compassionate. But we continue to ignore the true roots of their condition, roots that branch into our worlds and are nourished on our political and religious beliefs.

Until we radically alter our educational system, and solve the problems of poverty and social deprivation, our children will continue to spiral down stairwells of suffering and oppression.

As a group, blacks are only slightly less likely to single out individualistic factors in the cause of poverty than whites, but at the same time, blacks embrace structural explanations much more forcefully. Much more than whites, who favor individualist explanations in greater numbers, blacks embrace both explanations of poverty. This intriguing set of beliefs among blacks challenges flat either/or thinking, and may suggest why black views on the causes of poverty are more complex than usually allowed for. It is clear from social science research that many black folk are capable of sustaining two apparently contradictory views: recognizing that individual responsibility for personal destiny is enormously important to the culture, while at the same time acknowledging the structural barriers that prevent both social justice and self-realization.

The conflicts among northern blacks of different classes in the early twentieth century were nearly as bruising as those between the races, blasting the delusion that, before segregation's demise, black folk of every station were knit together in harmony.

The black poor, like most black people, have a more sophisticated and perhaps more complex understanding than we might imagine about how they have come to be poor and what they must do about it. Many black poor share some of the same values that motivate many in the mainstream — hard work, when they can get it; the desire for their children to prosper; the dream of upward mobility; and the soulful embrace of decent living.

Most successful black folk appear to recognize that while they have worked hard, applied themselves diligently, and taken advantage of every opportunity to enhance their God-given talents, that other black folk may not be as fortunate as they are in realizing their educational and employment aspirations. This sensitivity to less fortunate members of the race counteracts the beliefs of those who lean far too heavily on individual responsibility to explain social status. Since the bulk of blacks embrace structural explanations for poverty while leaving room for personal agency — and while the black poor themselves often seek to exercise individual responsibility in the midst of incredibly difficult circumstances — it stands to reason that fortunate blacks have a responsibility to acknowledge that complexity in defending the most vulnerable of the race. This holds even for conservative members of the race. Although new-fangled black neoconservatives have often forgotten this lesson, black conservatives from the past were more willing to acknowledge structural barriers while emphasizing personal initiative.

––––––

The need for loud lectures about hard work and personal initiative is vastly overplayed, more an instance of the lecturer needing to prove he is willing to take the poor to the woodshed than a case of the poor forgetting to do everything they can to escape poverty.

––––––

To adapt an old saying in black America in explaining the relative impact of social forces, if well-to-do-blacks have a cold, then poor blacks surely have pneumonia.

––––––

To paraphrase Dorothy Day, the great Catholic social activist who spent her life working with and loving the poor, but not pitying them, we must work toward a world in which it is easier for the poor to behave decently.

Exercising personal responsibility cannot prevent the postindustrial decline in major northeastern cities, nor can it fix the crumbling educational infrastructure that continues to keep the poor, well, poor. Being personally responsible can't stop job flight, structural shifts in the political economy, the increasing technological monopoly of work, downsizing, or outsourcing, problems that middle-class folk, who are presumed to be more personally responsible than the poor, face in abundance these days.

Even if they gave money to help hurricane survivors, a lot of rich people back East felt that the poor in New Orleans got that way because they didn't work hard enough not to be poor. But when the bottom fell out of Wall Street in 2008, when greed and horrible investment decisions caused huge financial harm to markets and to millions of investors, they got an up-close look at how easily, and unexpectedly, your economic life can be ruined. A lot of folk lost their shirts because of Wall Street bankers. There wasn't much talk about personal responsibility for those who were affected; there was instead a great deal of sympathy for their plight, unlike the sometimes mean-spirited attacks on poor blacks and Latinos who lost their houses in the subprime mortgage scandal. Let's be real: Wall Street couldn't understand the poor of the Delta until devastation dropped on New York's financial district out of nowhere. They couldn't understand the language of natural disaster, so it got translated into the grammar of economic devastation. That was their Hurricane Katrina!

I'm glad when my conservative brothers and sisters become concerned with the class issue and economic inequality. I'm all down for the class issue. But don't say class *or* race; say class *and* race. Let's yoke them together and then begin to do a deep thing: if we get poor white folk who have been excluded from American society to join with African Americans and Latinos and Native Americans — *we can turn this mother out!*

A date with a prison cell is greatly increased for poor folk stuck in poor schools.

Too often, poor people don't have the opportunity to exercise responsibility. Let me give you an example. I'm here in New Orleans, where I've been since last Friday, arguing, speaking, and participating in events to mark the one-year anniversary of Hurricane Katrina. And I've taken tours of the Lower Ninth Ward, looking at home after home. I see young black people and working black people saying, "Look, we have trucks out here. We want to go out and remove cars. They bid out the jobs, they prevent us on the local level from exercising our autonomy much less our responsibility." The government gave $100 million no-bid contracts to big corporations like Halliburton and Bechtel. So those who want to exercise personal responsibility are prevented by structural features like no-bid contracts, factors that prevent them from maximizing their potential. We will never be able to solve the problems of poverty unless we engage in less demonizing and stigmatizing of the poor, and begin focusing on the structural features — as well as the personal habits and dispositions that may perpetuate self-destructive behavior.

———

Even in the concentrated poverty of New Orleans, white brothers and sisters who are living in poverty don't live in the same kind of concentrated poverty that African American brothers and sisters live in. Which means, then, that there are some effects of poverty that are exacerbatory — that make it harsher for African American people who live under the ostensibly same conditions that white brothers and sisters live under.

———

There has been a shift, a subtle but very powerful one, from a war on poverty to the war on the poor. And the war on the poor that's being prosecuted, I think, is itself so deeply and fundamentally flawed that unless we withdraw from it, we will only perpetuate the devastation for the poor. Unless we're willing to say about the responsibility-versus-structural factors debate: "Hey, it's both/and, not either/or," we're not going to have a very enlightened conversation about poverty.

———

Poverty is the reason that in black neighborhoods some billboards promote higher-nicotine cigarettes, or that liquor ads are in poor black communities but not in rich white communities — or black ones, for that matter. It's why wealthier white and black kids come in from suburbia to try to get their "drink on" by going to the local liquor stores which dot the landscape of our communities like churches do. So it's about having a lack of political power to keep eyesores out of your community, or zoning laws that allow broken-down edifices and horrible houses to occupy your community. And then it's the downsizing and outsourcing and the capital flight, and the loss of nearly eight million jobs in the manufacturing industry. It's the exploitation of indigenous workers in foreign lands who will work far beneath a minimum wage as corporations flee the cities of our country in search of cheap labor and tax breaks on foreign soil — and you don't have a job. So when you put all that stuff together, you have a much different picture of poverty and the poor.

When you're poor, you often can't afford a washing machine. So you try to go to the Laundromat to get your clothes clean. But some people can't even afford the transportation cost to get to the Laundromat, so they get these rent-to-buy machines that are so costly. And yet, they're not cost effective. But poor people are caught betwixt and between. They don't often have a ride to the grocery store, so they have to ride with somebody else by giving them money. They can't take public transportation to take care of their basic needs. The predicament of poor people makes them so vulnerable — they're buffeted by all these economic and social forces.

Of course, personal responsibility is critical; good behavior is its own reward, because it gives you a sense of doing the right thing in the world. And most poor people we know behave right. But good behavior will not address all of the other factors that keep people poor, and that make them poor to begin with.

Working poor people often rise up early every day and often work more than forty hours a week, and yet barely, if ever, make it above the poverty level.

The black poor consists of the desperately unemployed and underemployed, those trapped in underground economies, and those working poor folk who slave in menial jobs at the edge of the economy. The black poor is composed of single mothers on welfare, single working mothers and fathers, poor fathers, married poor and working folk, the incarcerated, and a battalion of impoverished children.

There were virtues to the old southern geographies that formerly dominated black life. In the South, even if they were poor, black folk had open spaces in fields, but in the North, their enhanced economic status confined them in tenements that stretched upward several stories and choked the landscapes and skylines of ghettoes and slums.

The black ghetto working class, the working poor, and the permanently poor have always been more complex, and more resilient, than they have ever been given credit for.

Conservatives like Charles Murray contend that if we could somehow improve poor black women's initiative, their will to upward mobility, we could solve the problem of a congenital welfare syndrome. Most conservative analyses of welfare dependency and initiative are notoriously one-sided, neglecting the structural factors that prevent black women from flourishing. Initiative often depends on the amount of reward one receives for it. One's motivation to continually seek employment will not be high when there is little prospect of finding it. To help explain initiative, we must investigate the social causes behind the fragile place of poor black women in the economy; understand the sexist employment force, in which women continue to earn only seventy percent of what men make for comparable work; and measure the dominance of the service industry over manufacturing, which has eroded the wage base of poor black women, compromising their ability to support their families. Further, we must admit that a lot of female labor is chronically casual and acknowledge the disincentive of regulations that bar women from supplementing their welfare incomes with work. All of this cautions against simpleminded workfare solutions that tie welfare benefits to employment.

The shift of the labor base of black males from high-wage, low-skill jobs to scarcer service employment; the expanding technical monopoly of information services; the part-timing of American labor (leaving workers without employee benefits); and the wrenching of the U.S. economy by crises in global capitalism all bode ill for black males. These changes, coupled with cycles of persistent poverty, the gentrification of inner-city living space, the juvenilization of crime, and the demoralization of poor blacks through cultural stereotypes of widespread loss of initiative, only compound the anguish of an already untenable situation for black males.

The unfortunate part of the ghetto experience, of course, is that material misery and economic deprivation bring psychic harm and spiritual hurt to so many black folk. For every person who gets out of the worst ghetto situations, there are many more people who remain trapped in its punishing grip. I certainly don't romanticize poverty or the ghetto, although I understand how they have come to be mythologized in many black narratives of survival.

What I mean by "bourgie" — which is a pejorative term shortened from "bourgeois" — is not simply middle class. I mean by bourgie the construction of a self-determined persona that is hostile to, and scornful of, ordinary black people. You can be rich and not be bourgie. Class in black America has been about more than how much money you make or how many stocks you have; it's also been about the politics of style. I think that those of us who are privileged have an absolute obligation to "give back" to the less fortunate. I think we are bound by blood, history, and destiny to our brothers and sisters, especially to those who will never know the privilege or positive visibility that many black elites enjoy. And we should cross all lines — sexual, economic, religious, gender, geographical, generational — in speaking for the oppressed. For instance, that's why I think it's incumbent on me as a heterosexual black man to speak against the bigotry and injustice faced by my brothers and sisters who are gay, lesbian, bisexual, and other-sexed. And it's equally important for educated, upwardly mobile blacks to not forget those who have been entombed in permanent poverty and miseducation.

I attempt as much as possible to engage everyday black folk struggling on the streets. I understand and feel what drives them. It reminds me of where I was as a poor black kid in Detroit, a teen father who was hustling, who was thought of as a pathologized, nihilistic youth. I try to bring that dangerous memory, deeply inscribed in my mind, body, and soul, into the classroom through my style of teaching and lecturing — very animated, emotionally present, deeply in tune with the currents of social misery — and by means of some of the subjects that I try to confront.

———

Compassion for the poor is the hallmark of true civilization.

MED

chapter 17

Wisdom

Events take on a second life when memory and
wisdom mingle to give purpose to the past.

Events take on a second life when memory and wisdom mingle to give purpose to the past.

———

I realize that the process of self-acceptance is a sign of our spiritual maturity. It takes profound moral wisdom to claim, with our own lives on full theological display, that what God made is good.

———

The past should be a fountain of wisdom and warning. It is inevitable that fictions attach to what used to be. But it is immoral to make those fictions the ground of harsh judgments of our children.

———

So many young black people are cut off from the political wisdom they might receive if older black people would sit down and talk to them, teach them, converse with them — and yes, learn from them.

———

Pride was widely denounced because it destroyed the cardinal virtues of courage, temperance, justice, and wisdom that buttressed the political order and made the good life possible.

———

I was drawn to Wednesday night prayer meeting because I was able to absorb the wisdom of the church's senior saints and gray-haired griots. In their collective testimonies and prayers and prefatory comments to the songs they requested us to sing, the elders gave a running commentary on the hidden injuries of race and class, and the enduring hope and love

that propelled them over these huge obstacles. When they
bore witness to the pains and pitfalls they had surmounted
through faith, they gave renewed poignancy to clichés like,
"God will make a way out of no way." It was the opportunity
to hear the rich and surprisingly varied voices of the sisters
that was the greatest appeal of prayer meeting. At prayer
meeting, old black women — or "sore-head sisters" as they
sometimes called themselves in playful self-deprecation —
thumbed through the Bible and unleashed from its pages
golden nuggets of insight that rivaled those of most preachers
I'd heard. And their homespun wisdom was endearing. "I was
so green, you could plant me in the ground and I'd grow," one
sister humorously remarked in recounting the naïveté that led
to a youthful error.

――――――――――

The debate about corporal punishment is raging in our nation. There used to be a belief that there was a racial divide on
these matters, at least when we were growing up. Black folk
in favor, white folk opposed. Even though I don't think it's that
simple (where one lives, either in the city or the suburbs, and
one's class identification are important too), I don't deny that
racial differences exist. Recently, though, I think the gulf between black and white views on child rearing has probably
narrowed. A new generation of black parents has questioned
and often rejected the wisdom of whipping ass. To be sure, you
still hear black folk saying, "The problem with white folk is
that they let their kids get away with murder, let them talk and
act any way they want to without keeping them in check." But
you also hear black parents and the experts they listen to arguing that corporal punishment encourages aggressive behavior, stymies the development of moral reasoning, hinders
self-esteem, and even causes children to be depressed.

A daughter of the black community, Jocelyn Elders, attempted to bring the sharp insight and collective wisdom of our tradition to a nation unwilling to ponder its self-destructive sexual habits. Let's hope that her advice about the virtues of autoeroticism won't be lost on those closer to home. Like Marvin Gaye, black churches and communities need sexual healing. If we get healed, we might just be able to help spread that health beyond our borders.

Mature men temper strength with wisdom and know how to share power.

As a former resident of the ghetto, I wholeheartedly concur with the notion that we can neither forget its people nor neglect its social redemption through strategic action. Further, I think it's beautiful for folk who have survived the ghetto, who've gotten out, to carry the blessed image of its edifying dimensions in their hearts and imaginations, and to pledge to never leave the ghetto even as they travel millions of miles beyond its geographical boundaries. That means that they'll never betray the wisdom, genius, and hope that floods the ghetto in ways that those outside its bounds rarely understand. The ghetto is, after all, a portable proposition, a mobile metaphor. But we must not seize on the most limited view possible of ghetto life and sanctify it as the be-all and end-all of black existence. That leads to kids killing each other in the name of an authentic ghetto masculinity that is little more than pathological self-hatred.

We must remember orphaned and foster children who are robbed of the intimacies of family love and bereft of the benefit of parental wisdom.

In his book *Best Intentions: The Education and Killing of Edmund Perry*, author Robert Sam Anson sees Veronica Perry's swing from profound belief in the wisdom of God in taking her son to a bitter denouncement of the police system that killed him as a possible indication of her emotional instability. (She had had a nervous breakdown.) In fact, her "mood swing" may be understood as ad hoc theodicy, an attempt to come to grips theologically as best she could with the evil that killed her child. It is an attempt to vindicate — through faith — belief in a good and loving God who may appear absent or silent in the face of human suffering, without at the same time excusing the human beings who inflict that suffering. It is a theme that runs through the African American religious engagement with the world, and it is a central problem in Christian theology.

One of the reasons we suffer is because we ignore the wisdom of our women.

As debates about the literary canon continue, and as currents of suspicion about the wisdom of multiculturalism swirl, the example of black culture's constant evolution and relentless self-recreation is heartening. At its best, African American culture provides an empowering model of education that combines the desire for broad learning and the hunger for new forms of cultural expression. The ongoing controversies generated by identity politics, hip hop culture, and racial politics, and the rise of a host of other minority voices, means that African American intellectual life will remain vibrant as it helps to redefine American literature and democracy.

———

As a twenty-four-year-old pastor in Tennessee in the early '80s, I tested the black church's theological apartheid: I urged my congregation to ordain three women as deacons. One Sunday after I finished preaching, a deacon suddenly jumped to his feet and led the congregation in a vote to oust me, and for one of the very few times in my life, I was crushed to complete speechlessness. I had "swallowed my voice," in Marcia Dyson's eloquent phrase. I was fired with a month's severance pay and nothing else to support my wife and five-year-old son. I cried angry tears and packed my bags and found my way back to school to complete my degree in philosophy. But the lessons I learned as pastor of Thankful Baptist Church — the irony singes me to this day — are ones that I have never forgotten: that change takes time, especially yours if you're deeply invested; that black folk who are oppressed by racism readily turn to the same arguments used to keep them down to oppress women; that many women are hard-pressed to find the moral and social support to rebel against their own suffering; and that the black church is often the ground of our liberation and the soil that nurtures our most enslaving bigotries.

———

We are under judgment ourselves if we do not preach the gospel. If we are not being responsible for what God has given to us, we are sinning ourselves. And that means we have to sometimes oppose the wisdom of the world. Sometimes, like

Representative Barbara Lee, you've got to stand up by your-self. It looks like nobody else is going to help you; nobody else is with you. Even your former allies think you're crazy for what you're doing. But if God has told you to do it, you've got to stand up to do it.

The independent black press preserves the cultural and racial wisdom of black folk away from the glare of main-stream media.

Fannie Lou Hamer claimed that the mistake white folk made with black folk is that they put us behind them, not in front of them. Had they placed us in front of them, they could have observed and contained us. Instead, white folk placed us behind them in what they deemed an inferior position. As a result, we were able to learn white folk — their beliefs, senti-ments, contradictions, cultures, styles, behaviors, virtues, and vices. Black survival depended on black folk knowing the ways and souls of white folk.

The Cosby Show, in many respects, was a televised display of wisdom about adults and adolescents where the philoso-phies of Benjamin Spock and Marshall McLuhan easily em-braced. Cliff, an obstetrician, and Clair, a lawyer, were an exemplary dual-career couple. They smoothly melded tradi-tion and change. They offered their family tender devotion and tough love. Cliff and Clair blended parental authority, and adolescent freedom and responsibility, in perfect mea-sure.

The biggest knock on hard-core hip hop may be its tired, cliché-ridden exploration of violence, a subject that demands subtlety, artistic courage, and the wisdom to refrain from using a sledgehammer where a scalpel will do.

What is especially appealing about theologian Dwight Hopkins's lucid explanations of black religious belief is his grounding in the wit and wisdom of his forebears. Hopkins has never been afraid or ashamed to delve deeply into the folk genius of black culture, whether it surfaced in a slave narrative, a backwoods sermon, or the earthy eloquence of a community elder.

Malcolm X experienced profound personal and ideological changes near the end of his life. That inspired him to write an autobiography which viewed his life through a mythology of metamorphosis that led to spiritual wisdom.

To hear legions of black adults tell it, there was a time when a black child could be disciplined by any adult in the neighborhood if he or she did wrong. Such a story is meant to show the strength, unity, and durability of black communities of the past. It is also meant to underscore the weakness, fragmentation, and collapse of black communities today. Once, however, when I visited a university to lecture, I heard this same story repeated by a black youth, all of eighteen years old, who included her generation among the duly disciplined children. Most blacks would say that her generation is unfamiliar with such an experience. That gave me a clue that such stories are, in large part, rhetorical devices that transmit folk wisdom from one generation to the next. Such stories help us define the limits of acceptable behavior.

All in the Family showed us that Archie Bunker was the real dupe because of his bigotry. Archie's wife, Edith, was superficially daffy but revealed humanity and wisdom beneath her character's loopiness.

Names influence events.

For the victims, and survivors, of Hurricane Katrina, black faith refuses to offer pat answers or theological clichés. It is a tragedy of untold proportion, a catastrophe that causes the heart of God to break. And while the survivors are surely blessed, we must resist the notion that they are better than those who died. Black spiritual wisdom cautions against such presumptuous faith that feeds on pride. It helps us to resist the temptation to ethical arrogance. Those who lost their lives were victims of a force of nature that might have as easily drowned those who escaped. This is one of the paradoxes of black faith that we must not let collapse into black-and-white theological certitude: Yes, God's grace spared the survivors, but that doesn't mean that they are superior. The survivors are, therefore, charged with responsibility to live even more fully and purposefully in the awareness of their mysterious fortune.

How much wisdom could one expect from an artist like Tupac who barely lived beyond his twenty-fifth birthday, even though he was hugely talented and precocious to a fault? It is a testament to his gargantuan gifts — and to our desperate need, which screams so loudly because of our failure to find answers to pressing issues — that the expectation existed at all.

———

Black youth summon funeral directors to portray their dead bodies with a style that may defeat their being forgotten and that distinguishes them from the next corpse. If these youth are cynically viewed as the canary in the coal mine — since we all die, and death really is the mark of life, their actions embody the route we all eventually take to prepare for our demise — the sacrifice of their bodies for spiritual wisdom is a symbol of our inhumanity. Even if our reasons for allowing their suffering are not nearly as callous as that, the culture of death that suffocates black youth is nonetheless damning.

———

One of the things that black people have been afraid of admitting is that some of this stuff we deal with can make you lose your mind. You know, we have songs, like the one by DMX with the famous refrain, "Y'all gon' make me lose my mind, up in here, up in here." But the reality is that there's a great deal of mental stress for black men who want to fulfill the demands of a culture that tells us to walk, and then cuts our legs off. Black men are often left in tiny spaces to negotiate our psychic pain. That's why our suffering often opens up as wounds in public for the world to see. We don't get much private therapy and relief from the agony. We don't often turn to another brother to seek counsel and wisdom and direction. There are few spaces for everyday black men to do that. There appear to be even fewer spaces for well-known black men to heal from punishing situations.

———

Bill Maher is one of the bravest and most brilliant social critics we have in the aftermath of 9/11. Not only is he willing to challenge received wisdom on political practices and public policy, but he is capable of self-criticism, a rare trait among contemporary pundits.

———

One of the things I've tried to do in my work on the poor is to suggest the common sense and wisdom of black people who hold that if you're in the middle class, you ain't but a paycheck or two from poverty yourself.

———

Since I've been booted out of the pastorate of a black church for attempting to ordain women, and given that my extremely liberal views on homosexuality run counter to the received wisdom of many black theological lights, I must confess that my version of the faith might provoke as many cries of heresy as it may win converts.

———

Before Martin Luther King was baptized in the waters of liberal white theological education, he drew deep from the well of wisdom contained in the words of his church elders. King also learned the art of masking hard truth in humor. And he learned how to dress cultural observation in the colorful cadences of tuneful speech.

———

Outkast is among the most progressive and culturally sensitive hip hop groups now recording, one of the few rap groups that perhaps knows or even cares who Rosa Parks is or what she accomplished. Their song "Rosa Parks" invokes her presence as a metaphor for insight and wisdom, as a cautionary tale against an uninformed obsession with the past. They also appeal to her symbolic presence to warn all pretenders to their rap throne that they would have to move to the back of the bus — in other words, that they would have to take a backseat to Outkast's preeminence. In the world of hip hop verbal battles, that is indeed a gentle boast.

Martin Luther King was at his best when he was willing to reshape the wisdom of many of his racial and national parents. He ingeniously harnessed their ideas to his views to advocate sweeping social change.

One form of rhetorical resistance that has been prominently featured throughout black cultural history is the black sermon, the jewel in the crown of black sacred rhetoric. Here, a minister, or another authorized figure, thrives in the delivery of priestly wisdom and prophetic warning through words of encouragement and comfort, of chastening and challenge.

Malcolm X was the rap revolution's rhetorician of choice in hip hop's heyday, his words forming the ideological framework for authentic black consciousness. His verbal ferocity was combined with the rhythms of James Brown and George Clinton, the three figures forming a trio of griots dispensing cultural wisdom harnessed to polyrhythmic beats.

By choosing to honor the memory of Emmett Till, we make a covenant with our past to own its pain as our responsibility, and to forgive its failures only if the wisdom we gain in the process is made a part of our present pacts of racial peace.

Tell the truth gently.

MED

Photography Credits

Acknowledgments

As usual, I want to thank Liz Maguire, my beloved late editor, whose intellectual partnership and inspiration are all over these pages. I want to thank publisher John Sherer at Basic Civitas for his insight and good humor in supporting this book and my work. I am also grateful to Robert Kimzey, Michele Jacob, Mary McCue, Caitlin Fitzpatrick, and Jocelyn Giannini at Basic for their good work. I am especially grateful to the wonderful Nicole Caputo for her inspired cover design and to Rick Schwab for his great cover photos. I am thankful as well to the marvelous Christine Marra, who did her usual excellent job in producing the book, along with her crack team of copyeditor Gray Cutler, proofer Jeff Georgeson, and designer/typesetter Jane Raese. I am grateful to the photographers whose excellent work appears in these pages: Monica Morgan (feel better), Louis Myrie, Darryl Turner, Johnny Nunez, Impact Photo/Joe Photo, Regina Fleming, Matt Carr, Mark Mehlinger, W. Hassan Marsh, Donna Payne, Garlin Gilchrist II, and Nancy Kaszerman.

I thank all the splendid folk at Georgetown for providing me incredible support for my work: President Jack DeGioia, Provost Jim O'Donnell, and all my colleagues in the Sociology Department. I am grateful to the amazing support of my assistant, Kirby Blem, and the support of the incomparable Derreck Brown.

I send mad love, as always, to Susan "Queen" Taylor and Khephra "Smooth" Burns. I owe a special shout out and mad love to Marva Smalls for your incredible support of my work, books, and intellectual vision (and to the amazing Stephanie Phelps, Barbara Furlow, and David Bruson — I still might try to steal them!), and to Ingrid Saunders Jones, Richard Plepler, Johnny Furr, Mike Bantom, and Ken Chenault for your un-failing support over the years.

Finally, I am grateful to my family: my mother, Addie Mae Dyson, my brothers Anthony, Everett (we're getting you out soon), Gregory, and Brian. And my gratitude goes to my children Michael Eric Dyson, II (who's still riding solo!), Maisha Dyson-Daniels and Cory Daniels (and Layla Ophelia Rose Daniels), and Mwata Dyson (and little Mosi Izaiah Ayomide Dyson, welcome to the world). And above all I have love and gratitude for Rev. Marcia Louise Dyson and her unstinting loyalty and love, and for her profound commitment to humanity.